HOME GROWN GARDENING

BEST ROSES, HERBS, AND EDIBLE FLOWERS

HOME GROWN GARDENING

BEST ROSES, HERBS, *and* EDIBLE FLOWERS

EASY PLANTS FOR MORE BEAUTIFUL GARDENS

Houghton Mifflin Harcourt

BOSTON NEW YORK 2019

CONTENTS

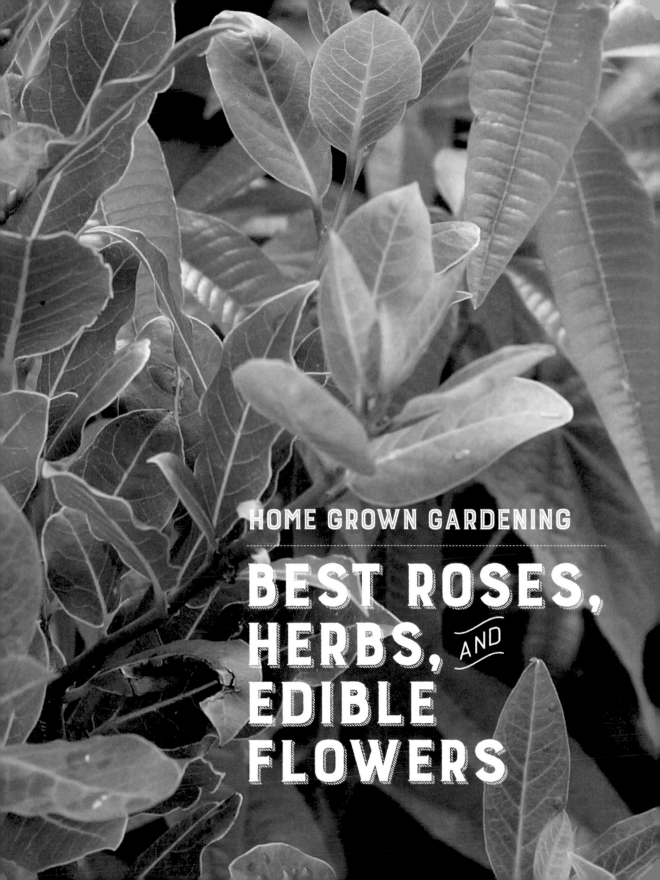

HOME GROWN GARDENING

BEST ROSES,
HERBS, *AND*
EDIBLE
FLOWERS

INTRODUCTION TO ROSES

Roses represent love and beauty. Their colors and fragrance create the standard by which many other flowers are measured. Cultivated around the world for perfume, roses have a sweet and unforgettable scent. Yet many would-be rose gardeners believe they require constant care: pruning, deadheading, training, feeding, and lavish doses of sprays and chemicals. Roses do require attention, particularly the hybrid teas, but their glorious flowers make all your efforts worthwhile.

The roses in this book were chosen because they are tried-and-true performers under the conditions stated with each selection. Their flowers are lovely, each with a distinctive character and some with fragrances that linger in your memory long after the last rose of autumn has faded away.

the world of roses

To simplify your understanding of this large and variable family of flowers, the featured roses have been divided into six groups.

SPECIES ROSES grow naturally in the wild. Typically, they produce flowers with five petals and come true from seed. They tend to be vigorous, ranging plants, ideal for settings where you want them to spread out and fill with blooms.

SHRUB ROSES is a class for roses that don't fit into the other groups. Some were bred by crossing sweet-scented, many-petaled old garden roses and more recent hybrid teas or other modern roses. In this category are ground-cover roses, hybrid rugosa roses, English roses, and others.

OLD GARDEN ROSES are those that were grown in the nineteenth century and earlier; they were mostly cultivated before 1867, when the first hybrid tea rose was developed. They are further subdivided into approximately thirteen classes, including gallica, alba, Bourbon, tea, damask, and centifolia. Usually they bloom once each growing season, in early summer, finishing before the onslaught of Japanese beetles that devour other roses in much of the country.

FLORIBUNDAS, GRANDIFLORAS, AND HYBRID TEAS

are popular rose groups. While the bushy, cluster-flowering floribundas and grandifloras are a fairly recent development, hybrid teas date back to the mid-eighteenth century. Hybrid tea roses are prized for their elegant high-centered blooms, long stems, and wide choice of colors, as well as their often delightful fragrance.

CLIMBERS AND RAMBLERS, with training, can grow over trellises, arbors, and buildings. They can also stand alone to form a lush free-form mound.

MINIATURE ROSES are very small. While a climbing miniature rose may reach 10 feet tall, the typical mini is 8 to 24 inches high. The flowers, leaves, and even thorns are all in scale with one another.

how to use this book

Let the pictures that follow inspire you to grow roses of your own. Or, if you already grow roses from one or two categories, study the entries for unfamiliar plants and try something new. Why garden, after all, if you can't have fun?

Whichever rose you choose, whether it climbs over an arbor or edges a little flower bed, savor it. Learn about roses firsthand by growing them, nurturing them, moving them when they do not thrive, and replacing them if they die, all the time increasing your knowledge of and joy in what many consider the most perfect of flowers. Included in the account for each kind of rose is information about the necessary growing conditions and vital statistics, as well as bloom time, using the designations common to reference books, rose nursery catalogs, and plant tags. Naturally, the exact date or month varies depending on where you garden and that year's weather conditions.

CARING FOR YOUR ROSES

Individual growing requirements and suggestion for care are included with each rose, but there are some general cultural and maintenance procedures that apply to all roses.

EARLY: This means the rose blooms in late spring or early summer.

MIDSEASON: The rose begins blooming in early to midsummer.

ALL SEASON: It blooms continuously, from early summer through fall.

siting

Take into account the shade tolerance, height, and width of the roses you choose to grow. Leave room for the shrubs to mature.

preparing the hole

Dig an ample hole, 2 feet wide and deep (somewhat less for smaller plants), and amend the soil with compost, well-rotted manure, leaf mold, or store-bought humus. If you're inclined to measure, use at least one part organic material to two parts soil. If your soil is heavy with clay, use sand mixed with humus or crumbly rotted manure to increase the drainage. Add a couple of handfuls of bonemeal or superphosphate to the hole to promote root growth. To avoid compacted soil, don't plant your rose when the soil is wet.

PLANTING

For a bareroot rose, soak the roots of the plant in water at least overnight or for 24 hours. Then set it in the hole on a crown of mounded soil and spread out the roots evenly. For a containerized rose, pop it out of its pot and tease apart the roots, especially if they're congested. Put it in a hole that is larger than the pot it came in. In either case, cover the plant so the bud graft is buried under 1 inch of soil in northern areas; it should be about 1 inch above the soil surface in warm regions. With your hands, pack the soil around the base of the plant. Water deeply.

mulching

After planting, spread a 2-inch layer of mulch such as rotted manure or compost over the root zone to retain moisture and keep the soil cool. Renew in fall after the ground has frozen and again each spring when leaves begin to emerge.

FERTILIZING

Once established, mound composted manure around each shrub. You may also fertilize lightly with a complete rose food in spring as buds begin to break and again after the first bloom begins to fade.

pruning

Before bud break, remove dead, damaged, or crowded canes. Information about how much to prune the healthy canes of individual roses is noted with each entry; the best time is generally while the bush is dormant, in late winter or early spring. To shape a rose-bush, just trim the branch tips by making an angled cut ¼ inch above an outward-facing bud.

DISEASE CONTROL

Roses get mildew and black spot, among other maladies. Always remove and dispose of affected leaves and canes; in fall, rake and remove dead leaves from around the shrub. Spray susceptible bushes each spring just as leaves are emerging and again throughout the season as needed. See individual entries for specific information.

pest control

If you live in an area of lush lawns, then Japanese beetles may be a problem. Pick them off by hand in the cool of the morning when they won't fly away, dropping them into a cup of soapy water to drown them. Spray grassy areas with milky spore or predatory nematodes. Rose stem girdler is a small green beetle that lays its eggs near the base of rose canes. When the soft-bodied grubs hatch, they feed on the stems, causing a swollen area, sometimes accompanied by splitting of the bark. To control, promptly prune out and destroy infested canes.

COLD WEATHER

Determine the cold hardiness of the roses you like to see if they coincide with the area where you live. Most likely, your property has microclimates where tender plants can remain protected and relatively warm year-round, while others are fully exposed to the elements. In Zones 6 and north, protect roses from winter damage by mounding 12 inches of soil or mulch over the base of each plant in fall after the ground has frozen. The addition of rose cones, or straw and chicken wire, may also be warranted, and helps protect the plants from the devastating effects of freeze and thaw cycles. The following spring, do not bare the roses until danger of frost is past.

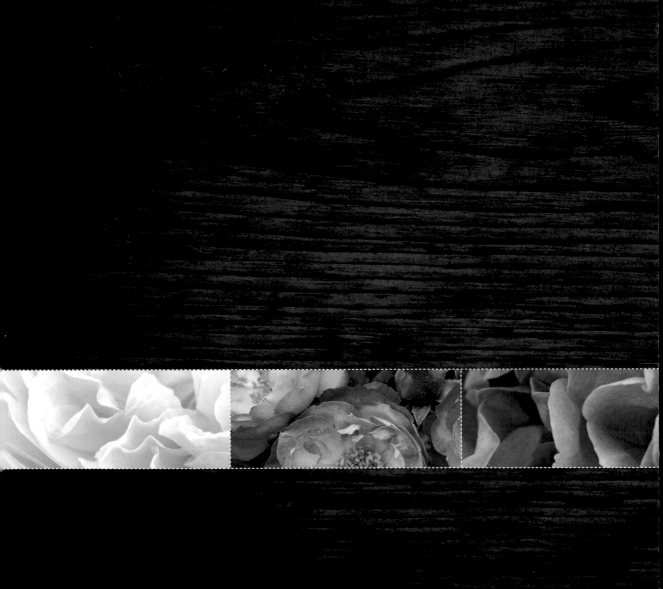

BEST
ROSES

APRICOT DRIFT

how to grow

Apricot Drift thrives in a site with full sun and fertile, moist (though not wet) soil, but it can adapt to average soil conditions. A yearly application of organic mulch, in a 1- to 2-inch-deep layer, helps to keep the roots cool and moist and discourages weed growth around the base of the plants. Prune the plants in later winter to early spring. They flower on new growth, so you can cut them back hard—by one-half to two-thirds—to promote vigorous growth and abundant flowering. Diseases rarely affect this easy-care rose.

With the time-tested favorite 'The Fairy' in its heritage, there's little wonder that Apricot Drift is an exceptional garden rose. The vigorous plants produce an abundance of clustered small buds that open to double flowers in shades of soft pink to peachy pink. When fully opened, the cupped blooms reveal a small cluster of yellow stamens in the center. They appear in a prolific first flush in late spring, with more flowers appearing through the rest of the growing season. As each flower finishes, its petals drop off neatly, so the plants stay tidy looking. Apricot Drift has a low, mounded growth habit and shiny deep green leaves.

ROSA 'MEIMIRROTE'

GROUND COVER

ZONES: 4–10
SIZE: 1–2 feet tall, 2–3 feet wide
BLOOM TIME: All season
BLOOM WIDTH: 1–2 inches
FRAGRANCE: Light
THORNINESS: Moderate

how to use

Classified as a ground-cover rose, Apricot Drift is obviously ideal for planting in masses, but that's just one way to enjoy it. Grow it singly or in groupings with perennials and shrubs in a mixed planting, use it as a low hedge, or plant it along the front of a foundation planting. In a container, its arching stems give the plant a cascading habit. Apricot Drift combines perfectly with blue- to purple-flowered companions, such as catmints (*Nepeta* spp.) and hardy salvias (*Salvia* spp.).

FLOWER CARPET SCARLET

how to grow

Like most roses, Flower Carpet Scarlet thrives in full sun and fertile, moist but well-drained soil. It can, however, adapt to a wide range of soil conditions, and it performs surprisingly well even in some shade, especially in hot-summer areas. To keep the plants vigorous and free-flowering, treat them to a generous layer of chopped leaves, composted manure, or other organic mulch each spring, and water during extended dry spells. Pruning is easy: simply cut all of the stems back by about half in late winter to early spring. Flower Carpet Scarlet typically shows excellent resistance to common rose diseases.

Flower Carpet Scarlet creates a glorious spectacle in the garden, carrying an abundance of flowers through the entire growing season—nearly year-round in mild climates. Held in clusters, the semidouble blooms are orangey red when newly opened, aging to brilliant scarlet and creating a dramatic contrast to the glossy deep green leaves. The plants have a low spreading habit and are practically trouble-free, making Flower Carpet Scarlet an excellent choice for any site where you need a showy, easy-care rose. Well known for its tolerance of heat and humidity, it's particularly good for southern gardens.

how to use

Classified as a ground-cover rose, Flower Carpet Scarlet truly does look terrific in a landscape setting: in space-filling masses, covering a slope, or as a street-side planting. It also pairs well with other plants, as an edging for a collection of shrubs, or combined with annuals and perennials in a mixed border or flower bed. It also works well in large pots, or even big hanging baskets, to decorate a deck or poolside sitting area. Flower Carpet Scarlet even makes a cute cut flower for indoor arrangements.

ROSA 'NOA8300B'
GROUND COVER

ZONES: 5–10
SIZE: 2–3 feet tall, 3–4 feet wide
BLOOM TIME: All season
BLOOM WIDTH: 2 inches
FRAGRANCE: Light
THORNINESS: Moderate

OSO EASY PAPRIKA

how to grow

Encourage healthy, vigorous growth and abundant flowering by giving Oso Easy Paprika a site with full sun and fertile, moist (but not soggy) soil. Each year, in late winter to early spring, trim out any dead, damaged, or crossing stems, then cut the remaining canes back by one-third to one-half. After pruning, spread a 1- to 2-inch-deep layer of composted manure or another organic mulch around the plants to promote good root growth and discourage weeds from sprouting. Oso Early Paprika generally shows good disease resistance but may be affected by black spot in some areas. If you notice dark discoloration on the leaves, pick off the affected foliage right away and spray the remaining leaves with a solution of baking soda and water to discourage further development of the disease.

The bicolor blooms of this gorgeous ground-cover rose are guaranteed to spice up your yard for months on end. Oso Easy Paprika provides a bountiful display of small clustered oval buds, which open into simple, single flowers with a yellow starburst in the center around a cluster of golden stamens. The main petal color is reddish orange on newly opened blooms, aging through coral- to peachy orange, giving the plant a multicolor appearance. The flowers appear in repeated flushes through the growing season over shiny, deep green foliage on spreading, mounded plants.

ROSA 'CHEWMAYTIME'

GROUND COVER

ZONES: 4–10

SIZE: 18–24 inches tall, 24–36 inches wide

BLOOM TIME: All season

BLOOM WIDTH: 2 inches

FRAGRANCE: Light

THORNINESS: Moderate

how to use

This versatile beauty offers lots of options. It's wonderful in small or large groups as a ground cover, of course: use it by itself to fill space on a flat or sloping site. It also looks great in a foundation planting or lining a path or walkway. In a mixed planting, it pairs perfectly with flowering partners in bright to pastel yellows or shades of blue and purple. Oso Easy Paprika adapts well to life in a large pot, too.

ROSA 'WEKSURDICLA'

GROUND COVER

ZONES: 5–10

SIZE: 1–2 feet tall,
3–6 feet wide

BLOOM TIME: All season

BLOOM WIDTH: 2–3 inches

FRAGRANCE: Light

THORNINESS: High

RAINBOW HAPPY TRAILS

how to grow

Full sun encourages the most prolific bloom in most areas, but if you live in a hot-summer climate, consider giving it a bit of afternoon shade to keep the flowers from bleaching out. Average to moist, well-drained soil that's enriched with organic matter is ideal. After planting, cover the soil around the plants with a 2-inch-thick layer of mulch to promote good root growth and discourage weeds. Water regularly for the first year and during dry spells after that. Rainbow Happy Trails naturally produces long, trailing stems, so it doesn't need much pruning; simply clip out any dead or damaged stems in late winter to early spring and snip shoot tips as necessary to shape the plants. Powdery mildew and rust usually don't affect this rose, but black spot may be a problem in some areas; spray with a mixture of baking soda and water to discourage disease development in humid climates.

If you're looking for a ground-cover rose but can't decide on just one color, take a look at Rainbow Happy Trails. This distinctive rose offers a variety of colors on just one plant, depending on the growing conditions. At the beginning and end of the growing season, when the weather is cool, the blooms appear nearly red with yellow centers. In warmer weather, the petals are bright pink at the tips and glowing yellow toward the base, often with a bit of white in between. The clustered oval buds open to cupped double flowers that appear in nearly continuous flushes throughout the growing season over glossy green leaves. Rainbow Happy Trails has a naturally low, spreading habit, making it ideal for use as a ground-cover rose.

how to use

With its multicolored flowers, Rainbow Happy Trails is eye-catching planted alone and spectacular in groups as a ground cover. Use it in masses to break up an expanse of lawn, let it trail over a retaining wall, or take advantage of its trailing habit to cover a hard-to-mow slope.

WHITE MEIDILAND

how to grow

White Meidiland can perform better than many roses in partial shade but is most vigorous, healthy, and free-blooming in full sun and fertile soil that is moist but well drained. After planting, water thoroughly and spread a 2-inch-thick layer of organic mulch, such as composted manure or chopped leaves, around the plants to retain soil moisture, maintain fertility, and discourage weed growth. White Meidiland generally needs little pruning, other than removing dead or damaged stems. If the dead flowers cling to the plant, use a leaf rake to knock them off. Disease resistance is generally good, but if you notice dark or powdery spots on the leaves, pick off affected parts and use preventive sprays (a mixture of baking soda and water) on the remaining foliage.

Meidiland roses are a time-tested group for landscape and garden use. The classic White Meidiland is blanketed with a bounty of oval buds, opening to fully double flowers held in large clusters. They are typically pure white but may be lightly blushed with pink, particularly in cool conditions. Most abundant at the beginning of the season, flowers can continue to appear until frost. They show off beautifully against the glossy, leathery deep green leaves. White Meidiland is on the larger side for a ground-cover rose, so it is ideal for larger landscapes.

ROSA 'MEICOUBLAN'

GROUND COVER

ZONES: 5–10
SIZE: 3–5 feet tall, 4–7 feet wide
BLOOM TIME: Midseason, with some repeat
BLOOM WIDTH: 2–3 inches
FRAGRANCE: None
THORNINESS: Moderate to high

how to use

If you have a large property, planting White Meidiland in masses is a great way to fill space with beautiful blooms. It also works well as a medium-height hedge or edging for driveways and wide walkways. In smaller yards, combine individual plants with other shrubs and perennial companions. Don't hesitate to snip some of the blooms for cut flowers, too!

ABRAHAM DARBY

how to grow

As with most English roses, a sunny location in good soil is best. Prune plants in winter in mild areas and early spring in northern zones. Cut the canes back by one-quarter for a more attractively shaped plant but fewer, smaller flowers. Abraham Darby is mildew resistant and mostly pest- and disease-free. It may show symptoms of rust in the East, Pacific Northwest, and mountain areas. To control, use a sulfur-based fungicide as needed. Always rake and remove dead leaves in fall.

Its large, spectacular blooms make Abraham Darby a must for any rose garden. The color is a soft, luscious apricot tinged with yellow on the inside petals and pink on the outer petals. The heady fragrance is soft and fruity. This rose was introduced by the English nurseryman David Austin in 1985 and named for a leader of Britain's industrial revolution. Abraham Darby blooms repeatedly until frost brings the show to a halt. The blossoms last a long time in a vase or bowl as elegant, perfumed centerpieces. Just beware of the thorns, which may grow to 1 inch long.

how to use

Abraham Darby is versatile in the landscape. Planted alone, it makes an attractive specimen planting. Planted in groups of three, it makes a dramatic garden statement since the individual plants will eventually merge into one large mass of leaves and flowers. To create this effect, stake out an equilateral triangle with 2-foot sides and plant one rose at each corner. This rose also works well in a mixed border or as part of a rose bed featuring different rose varieties.

If you lack the space for a shrub rose in your garden, plant this rose as a low climber. The arching stems of Abraham Darby can grow up to 10 feet tall when trained against a wall or trellis.

ROSA 'AUSCOT'

SHRUB (ENGLISH)

ZONES: 6–9
SIZE: 4–6 feet tall, 3–4 feet wide
BLOOM TIME: Summer to frost
BLOOM WIDTH: 5 inches
FRAGRANCE: Moderate
THORNINESS: Very

BEACH ROSE

how to grow

Rosa rugosa does best in full sun but also grows well in sites with some light afternoon shade. It thrives in adverse conditions, making it a good choice for areas with sandy soils, coastal gardens, or hot, dry sites. Plant in any well-drained soil. Fertilize by top-dressing with rotted manure in spring and again in fall. Shear a hedge or windbreak each spring. This rose is occasionally troubled by rose stem girdler (prune out and destroy infested canes) and Japanese beetles (handpick).

Rosa rugosa is a familiar sight along the New England coast. Some call it the beach rose because it thrives in harsh seaside conditions. Others say it's the Japanese rose because it originated in Japan (and in Korea and northern China). Most gardeners who grow this rose agree that, whatever its name, this rugged plant adds both heady fragrance and beauty to the garden. Perfumed blossoms of magenta-pink with five to twelve petals open from long, pointed buds. These repeat from spring until frost. Canes are thick, upright, and robust—and bristling with thorns. The dark green leaves are leathery and wrinkled with deep-set veins; they turn yellow in fall. The fat, round hips measure about an inch in diameter. This rose is disease-free and winter hardy to –50°F and stands up to 6 feet tall with a dense and spreading habit.

ROSA RUGOSA
SHRUB

ZONES: 2–9
SIZE: 3–6 feet tall, 6 feet wide
BLOOM TIME: All season
BLOOM WIDTH: 2–3 inches
FRAGRANCE: Strong
THORNINESS: Very

how to use

Because of its dense habit and its thick, prickly stems, *Rosa rugosa* makes an impenetrable hedge. It can also bring summer-long contrast and color to the typical foundation planting of conifers and broad-leafed evergreens. Rugosas are suitable for mixed beds and borders. They thrive in difficult conditions, such as near a busy road in poor soil with exposure to pollution, or in the path of harsh, salty winds at the seaside.

ROSA 'MEIDOMONAC'

SHRUB

ZONES: 4–9

SIZE: 3–5 feet tall,
5 feet wide

BLOOM TIME: Midseason,
with excellent repeat

BLOOM WIDTH: 2 inches

FRAGRANCE: None

THORNINESS: Moderate

BONICA

how to grow

Plant in full sun in well-drained soil amended with compost, manure, or leaf mold. Then add a layer of mulch 1 or 2 inches thick around the root zone. Prune in late winter or early spring while plants are still dormant. Prune hedges lightly, shaping the plants and removing damaged or old canes. Bonica contracts black spot if preventative sprays are not applied. Spray with a solution of baking soda and water for light infections. If the disease has gained a foothold, spray with a solution of fungicidal soap and repeat in 2 weeks.

This rose offers a big payoff for little work. Bonica is a healthy plant that blooms all summer long and is winter hardy to chilly Zone 4 (with protection). The flower's inner petals are medium pink, while the outer ones are a light silvery pink. Each double bloom has forty or more petals but barely any scent. The abundant flower clusters make a striking contrast with the small, dark green leaves against which they are set. These are followed in autumn by orange-red hips that, in many areas, persist well into winter. Introduced in France in 1982, Bonica became the first shrub rose to be named an All-America Rose Selection (in 1987) and won a German award for exceptional hardiness and disease resistance.

how to use

Bonica makes an excellent tall ground cover or landscape rose. Gardeners especially prize its ability to choke out weeds. Grown as a dense hedge or massed in beds, Bonica has an extended season of interest; after the blooming period has passed the plant sets attractive orange-red hips that last into winter. Bonica also makes a handsome addition to the mixed border or stands on its own as a garden specimen. It works well in small gardens, where every plant counts, because of its rather modest size and because its growth is easily kept in check. Its medium pink flowers harmonize well with silver-leafed artemisias and blue campanulas, delphiniums, or salvias.

CAREFREE WONDER

how to grow

Carefree Wonder prefers a site in full sun, and the more organic matter you can add to the planting hole, the better. It needs little or no pruning. Shape the plant a bit, if necessary, each spring before its buds begin to open. Japanese beetles are sometimes a problem; pick them off by hand and drop into a jar of soapy water. If you buy a commercial trap for Japanese beetles, set it up well away from your rosebushes so you don't inadvertently lure the beetles to your roses.

With medium pink petals, a creamy white reverse, and a white eye, each blossom of Carefree Wonder looks like a hand-painted work of art. Its double-cupped blossoms have twenty-six petals that appear singly and in small clusters; its scent is light and sweet. Winter-hardy Carefree Wonder is disease resistant and blooms continuously from midseason until frost. The neat but vigorous, bushy shrub has dense, semiglossy medium green foliage and reddish thorns. Bred by Meilland of France, Carefree Wonder captured the prestigious All-America Rose Selection Award in 1990.

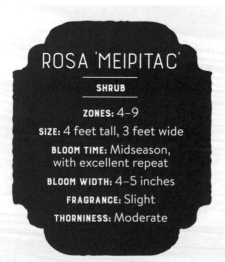

ROSA 'MEIPITAC'

SHRUB

ZONES: 4–9

SIZE: 4 feet tall, 3 feet wide

BLOOM TIME: Midseason, with excellent repeat

BLOOM WIDTH: 4–5 inches

FRAGRANCE: Slight

THORNINESS: Moderate

how to use

Because Carefree Wonder has a neat habit, it suits gardens of any size, an advantage for rose lovers with limited space. The shrub's trim growth and appearance make it appropriate not only for low-blooming hedges but also for foundation plantings. Massed in an uneven-numbered group, the floriferous Carefree Wonder provides a dramatic color accent in the shrub border. It also makes a nice stand-alone garden specimen.

CECILE BRUNNER

how to grow

'Cecile Brunner' prefers a site in full sun in northern areas and a sunny place with some light afternoon shade in regions where summers are hot. (Provide winter protection in Zone 5 and colder parts of Zone 6.) Plant in soil amended with organic matter to increase fertility and improve drainage. For best flower production, prune back canes by one-half to two-thirds when leaves begin to emerge in spring. To stimulate flowering, fertilize with a balanced rose fertilizer after the first flush of flowers and prune lightly to remove spent flowers. This rose may suffer from some black spot in summer. Apply a fungicidal soap or sulfur as the leaves emerge, and as needed thereafter. Its small leaves are subject to mite damage in late summer, especially when the weather is hot and dry. To control, spray plants with insecticidal soap, repeating every 7 to 10 days for a month.

Introduced in France in 1881, 'Cecile Brunner' is the classic, old-fashioned sweetheart rose. It bears perfectly formed flowers that begin as tiny, pointed light pink buds. When open, the small double blooms are lightly fragrant and look like miniature hybrid tea roses. They are borne first singly and later in sprays. 'Cecile Brunner' forms a bushy, rounded, spreading shrub with small, semiglossy dark green foliage that is dense and plentiful; plus it is nearly thorn-free. Because of the flowers' petite size, sweet smell, and smooth stems, 'Cecile Brunner' is the consummate buttonhole rose.

how to use

'Cecile Brunner' is a dwarf polyantha rose. Because of its small stature and tidy habit, it suits small gardens as well as large ones. The shrub's trim growth and appearance make it appropriate as a low-blooming hedge, as an edging, or massed in a small bed. You can also grow 'Cecile Brunner' in a pot, as long as you keep it well watered and fed.

ROSA 'CECILE BRUNNER'

SHRUB (POLYANTHA)

ZONES: 5–9
SIZE: 3 feet tall, 3 feet wide
BLOOM TIME: Late season, with excellent repeat
BLOOM WIDTH: 1½ inches
FRAGRANCE: Slight
THORNINESS: Slight

CHARLOTTE

how to grow

Charlotte thrives in the same conditions that most other roses appreci-ate: full sun with fertile soil that is moist but not wet. Each spring, cover the ground around the base of the plant with a 1- to 2-inch-thick layer of chopped leaves, compost, or another organic mulch to promote healthy root growth. Prune in late winter to early spring. First remove any dead, damaged, or crossing canes, then trim the remaining stems lightly to shape the plant. Charlotte generally has good disease resistance but may be bothered by black spot or powdery mildew in some climates. If you notice symptoms developing, remove affected parts right away and then spray with a mixture of baking soda and water to discourage further spread of these fungal diseases.

Bred by the renowned rosarian David Austin, this elegant English rose is a beautiful addition to sunny gardens. Its peachy orange buds open to buttery yellow blooms with outer petals that age to cream, giving the flowers a bicolor appearance, especially in warm weather. Held in small clusters, the fully double, cupped blooms are packed with petals and appear in flushes through the growing season over the leathery medium green leaves. Charlotte is classified as a shrub rose, with an upright, bushy habit.

ROSA 'AUSPOLY'

SHRUB

ZONES: 5–10

SIZE: 4–6 feet tall, 4–5 feet wide

BLOOM TIME: Midseason, with good repeat

BLOOM WIDTH: 3 inches

FRAGRANCE: Moderate

THORNINESS: Light

how to use

Enjoy Charlotte as a flowering hedge or tuck it into a mixed border with other shrubs and perennials. Its old-fashioned flower form also makes it look right at home in a cottage-garden setting. The plant can also adapt to life in a large container to dress up a deck, patio, or poolside. It looks particularly pretty with com-panions that bloom in shades of blue and purple, such as catmints (*Nepeta* spp.), hardy salvias (*Salvia* spp.), bellflowers (*Campanula* spp.), and pincushion flower (*Scabiosa columbaria*).

ROSA 'FRAU DAGMAR HARTOPP'

SHRUB (HYBRID RUGOSA)

ZONES: 3–8

SIZE: 2–4 feet tall, 4 feet wide

BLOOM TIME: Early to midsummer, repeat

BLOOM WIDTH: 3 inches

FRAGRANCE: Strong

THORNINESS: Very

FRAU DAGMAR HARTOPP

how to grow

Like other hybrid rugosas, this rose thrives in hot, dry conditions. It excels in problem areas where gentler plants may falter. Any spot in full sun with well-drained soil will do. Prune in late winter or early spring while plants are still dormant. Remove any dead or damaged canes and one or two of the oldest, thickest stems. Prune back the remaining canes by one-third. While the foliage is tough and disease resistant, rose stem girdler causes canes to swell and die. Control by removing infested canes as soon as they appear. Handpick Japanese beetles if they pose a problem.

Unlike many roses, 'Frau Dagmar Hartopp' ends the growing season with a bang. Its shiny, deeply veined dark green leaves turn deep reddish purple, then change to rich gold. Large, gleaming orange-red hips bring color to the garden in fall, when they take the place of faded flowers. The plant is small for a rugosa, and it may eventually grow wider than tall. Thorns in many lengths cover the entire cane. The flowers are intensely fragrant with the scent of cloves, and each has five light pink petals that form a saucer around creamy stamens. The first bloom comes in early- to midseason, and repeats until frost. A Danish hybrid introduced around 1914, 'Frau Dagmar Hartopp' is very winter hardy. (It is sometimes offered as 'Frau Dagmar Hastrup'.)

how to use

'Frau Dagmar Hartopp' is excellent sited near south-facing walls or beside a driveway where heat is reflected. Because it tolerates salt, it's a good choice for beach houses and gardens near heavily salted roads. Its low, thick, spreading habit and very thorny canes make it an excellent candidate for a short, impenetrable hedge. Space plants 2½ to 3 feet apart for a hedge or group planting. It also makes a handsome addition to a mixed border or can stand on its own.

GOLDEN CELEBRATION

how to grow

A site with plenty of sun and well-drained soil that's enriched with organic matter is ideal for Golden Celebration. After planting, mulch with a 1- to 2-inch-thick layer of an organic mulch, such as garden compost or composted manure, to promote healthy, vigorous root growth. Water thoroughly during dry spells. Prune in late winter to early spring, removing dead or weak stems and cutting the remainder back by one-third to one-half. If needed, you can prune again after the first flush of bloom, trimming the stems that flowered as needed to shape the plant. Golden Celebration typically shows good disease resistance but may be affected by black spot; use preventive sprays of baking soda mixed with water if needed.

Golden Celebration is a gem of a rose, combining the romantic charm of an "antique" rose with the reblooming trait of a modern hybrid. Rounded, pink-blushed buds, held singly or in clusters, open to fully double, cupped blooms that are tightly packed with silky petals. The large, delightfully fragrant flowers are golden yellow (particularly rich in color in cooler weather), aging to a softer yellow. Classified as a shrub rose, Golden Celebration tends to produce long, arching canes once it's established, often giving the plant a wide, fountainlike form. You can also use it as a "climbing" rose. Either way, it can grow significantly larger than many other shrub roses in mild-climate gardens.

ROSA 'AUSGOLD'

SHRUB

ZONES: 5–10

SIZE: 4–6 feet tall, 5–6 feet wide

BLOOM TIME: Midseason, with good repeat

BLOOM WIDTH: 4–5 inches

FRAGRANCE: Strong

THORNINESS: Moderate

how to use

Golden Celebration looks right at home in a cottage-style garden but also works well in a more modern mixed border with other shrubs, perennials, and ornamental grasses. Site it near a sitting area on a patio or deck, by a pool, or next to your favorite garden bench so you can enjoy the intense, sweet fragrance while you're relaxing outdoors. If you don't have room to let it spread, train it as a climber on a wall or large trellis, along a fence, or over an arch or arbor.

GRAHAM THOMAS

how to grow

Give this beauty full sun and well-drained, rich soil generously amended with rotted manure or organic matter. Add a layer of mulch at planting time and renew every spring and fall. Fertilize with a complete rose fertilizer in spring when the new leaves begin to emerge and again after the first flush of flowers. In late winter or early spring, cut the canes back by one-half to two-thirds. Prune again after the first bloom has faded to encourage rebloom. Trim any long canes that develop in late summer to keep the shrub well shaped. To control black spot, apply fungicidal soap when leaves emerge in spring and reapply as needed throughout the season. In Zone 5, the limit of its range, mound a 12-inch layer of soil over the base of the plant to protect it from winter damage.

The renowned English rosarian Graham Thomas chose this plant, introduced by David Austin in 1983, to bear his name. The flowers are an unforgettable rich golden yellow, full, and fragrant. Each bloom has thirty-five petals that retain the blossom's signature cupped shape until they fall. Austin described its tea-rose fragrance as slightly tarry, like the leaves of China tea. The deliciously pungent scent can suffuse a warm room.

how to use

'Graham Thomas' has a tall, narrow upright habit. If you live in an area with a long growing season, pruning the canes back hard (see above) may keep the plant shorter and the blooms lower on the stems. One bush makes an excellent addition to the mixed border, where its yellow, peony-like blooms can be appreciated with herbaceous perennials. Since much of this plant's energy goes into producing flowers and not into creating a dense shrub, a group planting creates a fuller look.

ROSA 'AUSMAS'

SHRUB (ENGLISH)

ZONES: 5–9

SIZE: 4–8 feet tall, 4–5 feet wide

BLOOM TIME: Summer, with variable repeat

BLOOM WIDTH: 3–4 inches

FRAGRANCE: Strong

THORNINESS: Moderate

KNOCK OUT

how to grow

Knock Out can be surprisingly adaptable for a rose, often tolerating somewhat shady sites and dry conditions. For the best growth and most abundant flowering, though, give it a site with lots of sun and fertile, well-drained soil. Give it a 1- to 2-inch layer of organic mulch each year, and water during extended dry spells. Knock Out looks best with yearly pruning—down to about 18 inches—in late winter to early spring. This rose tends to have good to excellent resistance to black spot and powdery mildew, so spraying is seldom necessary.

With their dependable, easy-care nature, the Knock Out family of roses has given confidence to many gardeners who thought they couldn't succeed with these supposedly finicky plants. They come in a range of colors now, but the original Knock Out is still very popular. Its semidouble flowers bloom in a vibrant shade of cherry red and hold their color well even in hot weather. They appear in a large flush in early summer, with somewhat smaller, repeated flushes until frost, so there are always some flowers to catch the eye. They show off well against the deep green leaves and may develop into small orange-red hips later in the season.

how to use

ROSA
'RADRAZZ'

SHRUB

ZONES: 5–10
SIZE: 3–5 feet tall, 3–5 feet wide
BLOOM TIME: All season
BLOOM WIDTH: 3–4 inches
FRAGRANCE: Light
THORNINESS: Heavy

Create a spectacle by planting Knock Out in masses to fill a large area, in groups in a foundation planting, or in a row as a flowering hedge. Or, use it to add spots of intense color among other plants in a shrub border or in a mixed border with annual and perennials. Partners with silver foliage, such as wormwoods (*Artemisia* spp.), provide an elegant backdrop for the rose's dark foliage and glowing blossoms. Consider flowering companions in bright white, sunny yellow, or rich purples for a stunning summer show. Hybrid daylilies (*Hemerocallis* hybrids) in a range of colors combine beautifully with Knock Out. This rose also works well in large pots.

MARY ROSE

how to grow

Mary Rose thrives in full sun in well-drained soil amended with lots of organic matter. Fertilize with a complete rose fertilizer in spring as buds begin to break and again after the first blooms begin to fade. In addition to routine pruning, deadhead (see page 118) to encourage repeat blooming in late summer. Mary Rose is more resistant to black spot than some other English roses, but the disease can appear during hot, humid summers. To control, apply fungicidal soap in spring as new leaves emerge. Reapply as needed throughout the growing season.

Mary Rose, introduced in 1983, looks like an old-fashioned charmer. Its compact, shrubby habit has an attractive fullness. Its loosely cupped rose-pink flowers recall treasured blooms of the past, and it has a pleasing light anise fragrance. Yet unlike many old garden roses that bloom once a year in June, Mary Rose blooms in early summer and repeats until frost. Its flowers are clustered on upright stems, and its leaves are large, shiny, and medium green. Vigorous, thorny canes take well to hard pruning or may be left long to form a bigger bush. Mary Rose is also disease resistant and winter hardy.

how to use

If you covet the grace and allure of old garden roses but lack the space for one, compact Mary Rose may be the answer. Because of its width, this rose is also suitable for planting side by side to form a low, thorny hedge. Mary Rose makes a handsome container planting on a patio or near a door, where its sweet, delicate fragrance can be appreciated. Plant one Mary Rose in a mixed border of shrubs and flowers, or create the effect of a large mound in the landscape by cultivating it in a group of three.

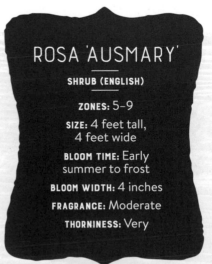

ROSA 'AUSMARY'

SHRUB (ENGLISH)

ZONES: 5–9

SIZE: 4 feet tall, 4 feet wide

BLOOM TIME: Early summer to frost

BLOOM WIDTH: 4 inches

FRAGRANCE: Moderate

THORNINESS: Very

MORDEN CENTENNIAL

how to grow

This tough rose thrives in a range of soils so long as they are well drained. Like other Morden roses, it prefers a site in full sun. Fertilize in spring as new leaves are emerging with a complete rose fertilizer. Prune in late winter or early spring, cutting back the canes by one-third to one-half to encourage heavy flowering and vigorous growth. 'Morden Centennial' is resistant to many pests and diseases, including black spot.

Gardeners in very cold climates will appreciate 'Morden Centennial'. This rugged rose survives temperatures down to −40°F. In summer it blooms prolifically, bearing lovely, fully double, medium pink blossoms. The cup-shaped, fifty-petaled flowers are lightly fragrant and are borne in clusters of up to fifteen. 'Morden Centennial' has an upright, bushy habit with semiglossy foliage. Its moderate disease resistance combined with plentiful midseason bloom and good repeat make it an excellent choice for gardens of the North. Introduced in 1980, 'Morden Centennial' was developed at the Morden, Manitoba, research station of the Canadian Department of Agriculture. Like the other roses in Morden's Parkland series, it is drought resistant enough to survive on Canada's semi-arid western plains.

ROSA 'MORDEN CENTENNIAL'

SHRUB

ZONES: 3–9
SIZE: 3–4 feet tall, 3 feet wide
BLOOM TIME: Midseason, good repeat
BLOOM WIDTH: 3–4 inches
FRAGRANCE: Slight
THORNINESS: Moderate

how to use

'Morden Centennial' is a hardy shrub rose, perfect for gardens with cold, windy winters. Because of its habit and a season of bloom that stretches almost 11 weeks, you can use it for a bushy, colorful, informal hedge. You can also mass it in a bed for a colorful focal point or use it in a mixed border with hardy perennials that have silvery foliage.

OLIVIA ROSE AUSTIN

how to grow

Olivia Rose Austin performs best with plenty of sun (perhaps a bit of afternoon shade in hot climates) in organically enriched soil that stays evenly moist but not soggy. A 1- to 2-inch-deep layer of chopped leaves, composted manure, or other organic mulch applied each spring will encourage good root growth, which in turn supports healthy growth and flowering. In late winter or early spring, prune out any dead, damaged, or crossing stems; trim the rest as needed to shape the plant and encourage branching. Olivia Rose Austin generally shows good resistance to common rose diseases, such as black spot and powdery mildew.

Bred by David Austin and named for his granddaughter, Olivia Rose Austin has a look of an "old" rose on a modern hybrid. This English rose produces plump buds that open into cupped blooms that are loaded with petals. The color is typically a light to medium pink but may appear nearly white in hot weather and strong sun. The fragrance is also variable—usually a moderate, sweet scent but can range from light to strong. The foliage is medium green and glossy. Expect to be patient with Olivia Rose Austin: the flowers can be small and loose on young plants but tend to improve in size and form over the first season, and in the years thereafter.

how to use

This English rose looks perfectly at home in a cottage-garden setting with classic perennial companions, such as lady's mantle (*Alchemilla mollis*), English lavender (*Lavandula angustifolia*), and pinks (*Dianthus* spp.). It also works well in mixed borders, where you could pair it with flowering shrubs, such as hydrangeas (*Hydrangea* spp.), and with perennials and annuals that flower in deeper shades of pink or white, soft yellow, or blue. Olivia Rose Austin can grow well in a container, too.

ROSA 'AUSMIXTURE'

SHRUB

ZONES: 5–10
SIZE: 3–4 feet tall, 3–4 feet wide
BLOOM TIME: Early to midseason, with good repeat
BLOOM WIDTH: 3 inches
FRAGRANCE: Moderate
THORNINESS: Moderate

RED-LEAVED ROSE

how to grow

Red-leaved rose is a sturdy, adaptable shrub. Full sun brings out its best leaf color, flowering, and fruit set, but it can also tolerate partial shade. Average, well-drained soil is fine. Little pruning is necessary. If you want to control the size or shape of the plant, cut out a few of the oldest stems at the base each year. Or cut all of the stems close to the ground in early spring every few years to completely renew the shrub (it will not produce flowers or fruit that year). Red-leaved rose is rarely bothered by fungal diseases.

Prized more for its foliage and fruits than its flowers, this is definitely a rose with a difference! Red-leaved rose does bloom, of course, with an abundance of small single, white-eyed pink blossoms in late spring to early summer. They're not around for long, though—usually just a week or two—and aren't fragrant. The plant is still colorful, though, with rich reddish purple new shoots that develop gray-blue leaves that are blushed with plum-purple, especially near the shoot tips and in cool weather. In summer, you'll start to notice the oval "hips" (fruits) developing, particularly as they start to turn shades of orange as the growing season winds down. The hips mature to scarlet and then red through the fall and often remain on the plant well into winter. Red-leaved rose produces long, arching canes, forming a large, mounded shrub.

ROSA GLAUCA

SHRUB

ZONES: 3–8
SIZE: 6–8 feet tall, 6–8 feet wide
BLOOM TIME: Early
BLOOM WIDTH: 1 inch
FRAGRANCE: None
THORNINESS: Light to none

how to use

This rose can fill quite a bit of space, so be sure to give it plenty of room. Use it as an informal hedge, alone or combined with other flowering shrubs, or in a large mixed border. Pair it with sizeable, sturdy perennials such as hybrid daylilies (*Hemerocallis* hybrids), Joe-Pye weeds (*Eupatorium* spp.), and purple coneflower (*Echinacea purpurea*). It also looks lovely with ornamental grasses, such as 'Karl Foerster' feather reed grass (*Calamagrostis* x *acutiflora*).

SALLY HOLMES

how to grow

'Sally Holmes' prefers a site in full sun, but it can also grow in areas that provide an hour or two of light shade. Give this rose organically rich soil and fertilize with a complete rose fertilizer when leaves begin to emerge in spring. Prune in late winter or early spring when the plants are still dormant. Remove thin or crowded canes, as well as old or damaged ones. 'Sally Holmes' may get black spot; apply a preventive spray of fungicidal soap as leaves emerge in spring. If Japanese beetles are a problem, hand-pick to remove them.

The vigor of its canes and the abundance of single blooms in its flower clusters make 'Sally Holmes' a memorable plant. The buff-colored buds open to five-petaled creamy white blooms with showy golden stamens. The slightly fragrant blooms appear in huge clusters of up to sixty. 'Sally Holmes' blooms all summer long and stands tall, though with a somewhat lazy, sprawling habit. Glossy green, leathery leaves cover this hale and bushy plant. Introduced in 1976, 'Sally Holmes' is disease resistant.

how to use

Its size, vigor, and abundance of continual blooms make 'Sally Holmes' an excellent rose for a large garden. Use it as a specimen or to add color all season to a large shrub border. Because some canes may reach a height of 12 feet, it can also be trained as a climber.

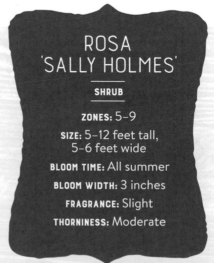

ROSA 'SALLY HOLMES'

SHRUB

ZONES: 5–9

SIZE: 5–12 feet tall, 5–6 feet wide

BLOOM TIME: All summer

BLOOM WIDTH: 3 inches

FRAGRANCE: Slight

THORNINESS: Moderate

THE FAIRY

how to grow

'The Fairy' grows and flowers best in full sun but does tolerate some light shade. Plant in a well-drained soil amended with some organic matter. Use a complete rose fertilizer in spring after plants have been pruned. In late winter while plants are dormant, remove one or two of the oldest canes; trim remaining stems back by about one-quarter. 'The Fairy' may get some black spot or powdery mildew in some years. To control, apply a fungicidal soap in spring as new leaves emerge, then repeat as required.

If you're looking for a rose that's practically guaranteed to thrive, try 'The Fairy', a favorite with gardeners since its introduction in 1932. Although this rose looks pretty and delicate, it's actually tough, disease resistant, and hardy to about −35°F without protection. The cupped, light pink flowers are small and cover the plant throughout summer and into fall. Each double blossom has twenty-four to thirty petals and grows in large flower clusters that, when cut, make handsome bouquets, though with little to no scent. The habit of 'The Fairy' is compact, tidy, and somewhat arching. Tiny, glossy bright green leaves cloak its moderately thorny canes. This versatile rose can also be grown as a standard for use in small gardens, to flank an entry, or as a focal point.

ROSA 'THE FAIRY'

SHRUB (POLYANTHA)

ZONES: 4–9
SIZE: 3–4 feet tall, 4 feet wide
BLOOM TIME: Summer, excellent repeat
BLOOM WIDTH: 1 inch
FRAGRANCE: None
THORNINESS: Moderate

how to use

Because of its neat habit and continual bloom, 'The Fairy' does well in pots, at the front of the border, or in small gardens with limited space. It makes an attractive ever-blooming hedge and an effective focal point when massed in the landscape. The compact habit and delicate flowers and foliage of 'The Fairy' complement perennials such as salvias and lamb's ears.

TOP GUN

how to grow

Optimal conditions for best growth and flowering are a site with full sun and fertile, well-drained soil. Water during dry spells. In late winter or early spring, prune out any dead, damaged, or crossing stems, then trim the remaining canes as needed to shape the plant. After pruning, spread a 1- to 2-inch-deep layer of an organic mulch, such as chopped leaves, composted manure, or garden compost, around the base of the plant to encourage good root growth and abundant flowering. Top Gun offers outstanding resistance to black spot, powdery mildew, and even rose rosette disease, so you don't need to think about spraying.

If you're looking for an eye-catching, easy-care rose, Top Gun belongs at the top of your must-try list. This superb shrub rose is in bloom through most of the growing season, with moderately fragrant, single to semidouble flowers held singly or in small clusters. The petals are a rich red hue and surround a boss of bright yellow stamens, creating a dramatic display against glossy, deep green, leathery leaves. Top Gun grows vigorously, with a bushy, somewhat spreading growth habit.

how to use

Top Gun is guaranteed to attract attention, no matter where you use it. It's particularly striking when planted in groups, or when used as a flowering hedge or as an edging along a driveway or in a street-side planting. It's excellent in mixed borders, too. Pair it with equally bright companions, such as golden yellow coreopsis (*Coreopsis* spp.) and orange coneflowers (*Rudbeckia* spp.), or orange-flowered zinnias (*Zinnia* spp. and hybrids) or cosmos (*Cosmos sulphureus*). It's very dramatic when combined with white flowers and white-variegated leaves, and with silver foliage.

ROSA 'WEKMORIDAHOR'

SHRUB

ZONES: 5–10

SIZE: 3–4 feet tall, 4–5 feet wide

BLOOM TIME: All season

BLOOM WIDTH: 3 inches

FRAGRANCE: Moderate

THORNINESS: Moderate

CHARLES DE MILLS

how to grow

Full sun is best. 'Charles de Mills' will, however, tolerate a few hours of light shade. It enjoys fertile soil and good drainage, but it will settle for slightly less if need be. Prune plants in late winter or early spring while still dormant. This rose can get powdery mildew late in the season; if so, apply fungicidal soap to the leaves.

The cupped magenta blooms of 'Charles de Mills', the largest-flowered gallica rose, are extraordinary for the number and organization of their petals. Numbering about two hundred, they are neatly packed and swirled in an arrangement that, when it is partly open, makes for a flower that is perfectly flat on top. Fully open, the blooms are ball shaped with a spot of light green deep in the center. Actual color may vary beyond magenta to crimson, wine, and violet. Blossoms are lightly scented and held high on their stalks. 'Charles de Mills', probably bred in Europe in the nineteenth century, is a shrub with thick, erect canes and some suckering. Canes may bend under the weight of the big flowers. Leaves are toothed, glossy, and dark green. 'Charles de Mills' is disease resistant and winter hardy.

ROSA 'CHARLES DE MILLS'

OLD GARDEN ROSE (GALLICA)

ZONES: 4–8

SIZE: 4–5 feet tall, 4 feet wide

BLOOM TIME: Midseason, with no repeat

BLOOM WIDTH: 3 inches

FRAGRANCE: Slight

THORNINESS: Moderate

how to use

'Charles de Mills' makes an attractive hedge; prune to shape in late winter or early spring, or leave unpruned for an informal look. Planted in groups of three, it creates a bold impact in the landscape when in bloom, particularly because of the way it holds its big blooms aloft. Silver- or gray-leaved plants contrast with the richly colored flowers and dark leaves, while plants with red or purple flowers harmonize with its floral tones.

STANWELL PERPETUAL

how to grow

'Stanwell Perpetual' prefers a location in full sun for best flowering but also does well with a few hours of dappled shade. Grow it in well-drained soil to which rotted manure, compost, or other organic matter has been added, spacing plants 4 feet apart. After planting, add a layer of organic mulch around the root zone. Fertilize with a complete rose fertilizer in spring when growth begins. Prune 'Stanwell Perpetual' in late winter or early spring when plants are dormant. Remove dead or damaged canes and trim remaining canes to shape.

'Stanwell Perpetual' has been a garden favorite since its introduction in 1838. This tough, hardy rose is one of the earliest roses to start blooming and one of the last to stop. Blossoms are a translucent blush pink fading to white, with forty-five to fifty-five petals. They open slightly cupped but flatten with age, the outer petals curving backward. Their lush scent is sweet and spicy. The flower's muddled center gives it a charming look of informality. Once firmly established in the garden, 'Stanwell Perpetual' is the only hybrid *spinosissima* rose that offers reliable repeat bloom. This rose has very thorny canes and small, fernlike dull green leaves. The bush is winter hardy and has excellent disease and pest resistance.

how to use

The only drawback to this lovely garden rose is a somewhat spindly habit. The late renowned English garden designer Gertrude Jekyll admired 'Stanwell Perpetual' and recommended planting three bushes together about 1 foot apart to create the effect of one large, full shrub. Such a group can work in a mixed border or alone as a specimen. Once established, 'Stanwell Perpetual' also makes a fine, long-flowering hedge.

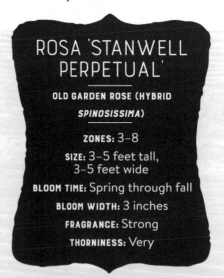

ROSA 'STANWELL PERPETUAL'

OLD GARDEN ROSE (HYBRID *SPINOSISSIMA*)

ZONES: 3–8

SIZE: 3–5 feet tall, 3–5 feet wide

BLOOM TIME: Spring through fall

BLOOM WIDTH: 3 inches

FRAGRANCE: Strong

THORNINESS: Very

TUSCANY SUPERB

how to grow

'Tuscany Superb' will tolerate some shade and less-than-perfect soil conditions and still bloom, but its dark color will lose its depth and fewer flowers will appear. It needs a site that offers fertile soil, good drainage, and plenty of water to perform its best. Pruning is minimal—after flowering is complete in summer, trim canes back by one-quarter. Occasionally black spot appears in late summer, but the disease does little damage. To control, rake up and discard fallen leaves in fall. Renew mulch around the base of the plant each spring and fall, and keep leaves as dry as possible in summer and fall.

'Tuscany Superb', a gallica rose, has large, fragrant blooms that are cupped, flat topped, and filled with velvety petals (between twenty-four and forty) the color of a dark wine or mulberry. Gold stamens add glowing contrast, though they are partly obscured by the ruffled effect of the inner petals. 'Tuscany Superb', probably bred in Europe in the nineteenth century, has thick, erect canes and suckering growth. With dark green leaves and plump, round buds, this rose makes an excellent garden specimen. It is both disease resistant and winter hardy, needing a period of winter dormancy to flower well.

ROSA 'TUSCANY SUPERB'

OLD GARDEN ROSE (GALLICA)

ZONES: 4–8

SIZE: 3–4 feet tall, 4 feet wide

BLOOM TIME: Midseason, with no repeat

BLOOM WIDTH: 4 inches

FRAGRANCE: Strong

THORNINESS: Moderate

how to use

'Tuscany Superb' makes an attractive hedge or landscape feature. Planted in groups of three, it creates a bold impact in the landscape when in bloom, particularly because 'Tuscany Superb' holds its big blooms aloft on strong stalks rather than letting them nod into the foliage. Planting 'Tuscany Superb' near shrubs with reddish leaves or red to purple flowers with a similar season of bloom brings out the depth and intensity of the rose's color.

ZEPHIRINE DROUHIN

how to grow

'Zephirine Drouhin' requires full sun and organically rich soil in a location sheltered from winds. It can be grown either as a large, sprawling shrub or trained to climb a support. As for pruning, before new growth begins each spring, remove a few of the oldest canes. Cut back remaining stems by up to half, leaving four or five vigorous buds per cane. Like most Bourbon roses, this one is susceptible to black spot. To control, apply fungicidal soap or garden sulfur to the new leaves in spring and repeat as needed throughout the growing season. Rake and dispose of dead leaves in fall.

'Zephirine Drouhin', a climbing Bourbon rose that dates back to 1868, produces cerise-pink blooms all season. The flowers are intensely fragrant, loosely cupped, and semidouble with twenty to twenty-four petals. Their vivid color stands out sharply against the semiglossy, medium green foliage, which is flushed with copper tones when new. 'Zephirine Drouhin' is a vigorous, well-branched plant with long basal canes that are nearly thornless along with short-flowering lateral canes. It is winter hardy only to Zone 6, and healthy except for an occasional problem with mildew.

how to use

Because the canes of 'Zephirine Drouhin' are mercifully smooth, you can plant it where you can appreciate both its looks and fragrance up close, such as adjacent to a walkway. You can also train it to climb a porch post, tree, or low wall. The long season of bloom (and few thorns) makes this a rewarding choice to flank a garden entrance. For large spaces, the bushes can be allowed to sprawl. Install a sturdy post on each side, or an arch, and train the two shrubs to grow vertically.

ROSA 'ZEPHIRINE DROUHIN'

OLD GARDEN ROSE (BOURBON)

ZONES: 6–9
SIZE: 8–12 feet tall
BLOOM TIME: All season
BLOOM WIDTH: 4 inches
FRAGRANCE: Strong
THORNINESS: Slight

AMERICA

how to grow

America needs at least 6 hours of sun per day to thrive, if not more. Plant in well-drained soil amended with organic matter. Once a plant is 3 to 4 years old, begin removing a few of the oldest canes annually in early spring. Cut back remaining ones to four or five buds. America can develop some black spot during wet, hot summers, and in the Pacific Northwest. Control with a fungicidal soap.

Notable for its dependable, all-season bloom, America is a large-flowered climber with double coral-pink flowers. Each bloom has between forty and forty-five petals and a potent, spicy fragrance. Flowers begin high centered but become cupped as they open. The habit of America is upright, spreading, and vigorous, and the foliage is medium green and semi-glossy. It blooms on old and new wood. The rose is tough, disease resistant, and winter hardy. America was an All-America Rose Selection for 1976, a designation earned by few climbers.

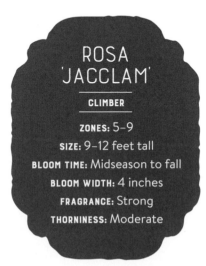

ROSA
'JACCLAM'

CLIMBER

ZONES: 5–9
SIZE: 9–12 feet tall
BLOOM TIME: Midseason to fall
BLOOM WIDTH: 4 inches
FRAGRANCE: Strong
THORNINESS: Moderate

how to use

America does well trained to grow up a trellis, wall, or arbor; just be sure to allow for some air circulation so it doesn't get mildew. (Install supports a few inches from a wall to allow air to circulate between the leaves and the wall.) Allowed to grow without support, the rose makes a sprawling hedge. Plant in groups to create a long-blooming mass of color in the landscape; a group makes a stunning cover for a large, sunny slope that you're tired of mowing.

BLAZE

how to grow

Plant 'Blaze' in full sun in well-drained soil amended with lots of organic matter. Once it is established (after the first 2 years), cut out weak climbing shoots that are no longer productive. After bloom, prune the lateral flowering shoots to the first set of five leaflets (about 3 inches long). Sometimes, however, you may want to train a vigorous lateral shoot to the framework to replace old, spent branches. Water consistently and deeply. Handpick Japanese beetles if they are a problem.

A first-rate performer, 'Blaze' (and 'Blaze Improved', pictured here) produces plentiful clusters of cupped, semidouble rich red flowers beginning in midsummer and repeating throughout the growing season. The blooms have a slight tea fragrance and up to twenty-four petals. Semiglossy medium green foliage creates the perfect backdrop for its abundant red blooms. Remarkably healthy and vigorous, this large-flowered climber deserves its popularity. It is disease resistant and winter hardy.

how to use

Because 'Blaze' grows quickly, has healthy and handsome foliage, and is a prolific bloomer, it makes an excellent choice for a trellis or a hedge. When planted as a climber, 'Blaze' makes a dramatic color impact in a small space. Plant several plants together to create a focal point in an expansive landscape. The flowers are splendid for bouquets.

ROSA 'BLAZE'

CLIMBER

ZONES: 5–9

SIZE: 8–12 feet tall

BLOOM TIME: Midseason, with excellent repeat

BLOOM WIDTH: 3 inches

FRAGRANCE: Slight

THORNINESS: Moderate

COMPASSION

how to grow

'Compassion' grows best in full sun in well-drained soil to which lots of organic matter has been added. For the first 3 to 4 years, the only pruning required is the removal of dead and diseased canes in late winter or early spring. After that, you may remove the oldest canes as well to keep plants blooming vigorously. 'Compassion' has excellent disease resistance. Slugs sometimes damage the young leaves. To control, spread a layer of diatomaceous earth around the plant's root zone or install a strip of copper around each plant. (Copper strips are available from garden centers and catalogs.)

Luxuriant blossoms and an award-winning sweet fragrance draw gardeners to 'Compassion', a large-flowered climber that grows as tall as 10 feet. The double salmon-pink flowers shaded with apricot are showy and large, with thirty-six petals. They occur singly and in small clusters and bloom lavishly throughout the growing season. Disease resistant and winter hardy, 'Compassion' has an erect, bushy habit. The canes have dark green semiglossy leaves and big red thorns.

ROSA 'COMPASSION'

CLIMBER

ZONES: 5–9
SIZE: 8–10 feet tall
BLOOM TIME: All season
BLOOM WIDTH: 5 inches
FRAGRANCE: Strong
THORNINESS: Moderate

how to use

'Compassion' is an excellent rose to grow up a pillar or pole. Because of its outstanding fragrance, site it where people can smell it, but not where its thorns would be a hazard. Keep it from encroaching onto paths or walkways so it doesn't snag people as they pass by. Try training it next to a porch or a window so you can enjoy its sweet scent indoors. It also makes a wonderful cut flower, thanks to its fragrance and elegant form. Grown unsupported, it makes a 7-foot-tall shrub; a row of this shrub makes a fine tall hedge.

DON JUAN

how to grow

Plant 'Don Juan' in full sun in rich soil amended with organic matter. 'Don Juan' is not reliably winter hardy; however, it is disease resistant and does well in southern climates. In Zone 6, site the plants near a south-facing wall for added warmth and winter protection. Do not prune 'Don Juan' after planting or during the first three seasons of growth. Once it is established, cut out weak climbing shoots that are no longer productive. After blooming, prune the lateral, flowering shoots to the first set of five leaflets (about 3 inches long). After a few years, leave one vigorous lateral shoot to train the framework to replace old, spent branches. 'Don Juan' has moderate disease resistance and can show signs of black spot and mildew in late summer. To control, apply fungicidal soap in spring as leaves appear. Repeat as needed until frost. Aphids and rose midge can be controlled with applications of insecticidal soap; handpick Japanese beetles.

Considered the best of the fragrant, dark red climbers, 'Don Juan' produces a profusion of large 2-inch buds and 5-inch flowers in velvety red when it first comes into bloom in midseason. The double blooms, which have a potent rose scent, have thirty-five petals arranged in a classic high-centered shape. The canes, 10 feet tall, are vigorous and erect, and the plant blooms on both old and new wood. 'Don Juan' has shiny, leathery dark green foliage—a stunning background for the blooms. Flowers have the best color where nights are warm.

how to use

'Don Juan' makes a handsome climber for pillars and trellises. It also makes an excellent hedge and looks good massed in the landscape. Because of its large flowers, heavy fragrance, and long 16-inch stems, 'Don Juan' is ideal for bouquets.

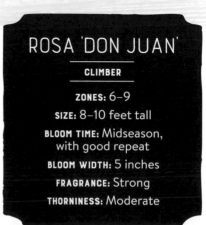

ROSA 'DON JUAN'

CLIMBER

ZONES: 6–9

SIZE: 8–10 feet tall

BLOOM TIME: Midseason, with good repeat

BLOOM WIDTH: 5 inches

FRAGRANCE: Strong

THORNINESS: Moderate

DORTMUND

how to grow

'Dortmund' thrives in full sun and well-drained, organically rich soil. For the first 3 years after planting, prune out only dead or damaged wood in late winter. Thereafter, you can begin taking out older canes, again while the plant is dormant. 'Dortmund' has excellent disease resistance and is usually not troubled by pests. It is one of very few climbers that are reliably hardy in Zone 4.

Introduced in 1955, 'Dortmund' was hybridized by Kordes, the German rose breeder who created several extremely hardy roses. A tough and hardy climber, it produces large clusters of splendid bright red flowers. They're single, consisting of five petals with a pure white eye and flashy gold stamens. The petals overlap, creating a ruffled contour, and the flower exudes an applelike perfume. Large hips appear after the flowers, but they should be removed early in the season to encourage further flowering. Later in the season, keep the hips for their handsome orange-red autumn show. The leafy canes are equally attractive. Leaves are dark green and shiny, and thorns on the new growth tend to be flushed with red. Winter hardy and disease resistant, 'Dortmund' has an upright, vigorous habit.

ROSA 'DORTMUND'

CLIMBER

ZONES: 4–9

SIZE: 10–12 feet tall

BLOOM TIME: Midseason, with good repeat

BLOOM WIDTH: 3 inches

FRAGRANCE: Moderate

THORNINESS: Very

how to use

'Dortmund' makes a dramatic impact on pillars and trellises as a climber. Its bold colors show up well from a distance, so this is a good rose for training up a sunny wall at the far end of a yard or garden. Although its scent is pleasing and its looks are sensational, avoid planting 'Dortmund' where you might inadvertently brush against its thorny canes.

FOURTH OF JULY

how to grow

For best growth and flowering, give Fourth of July a site with lots of sun and fertile, moist but well-drained soil, and treat it to a 1- to-2-inch-thick layer of organic mulch each year. Be aware that this rose can take a few years to settle in and start producing long, "climbing" canes. In fact, some people grow it as a large shrub, by pruning back the longest canes each year once they do appear. If you want to use it as a climber, let the long canes grow untrimmed and tie them to whatever support structure you've chosen. Once the plants are established, cut out one or two of the oldest canes at the base each year in early spring to stimulate vigorous new stems, then trim the side shoots on the remaining canes back to three to five buds to encourage good flowering. Fourth of July generally has good disease resistance, but you may need to apply sprays of baking soda mixed with water if black spot is common in your area.

Fourth of July rose is so showy that you can't miss it at a distance, but you'll want to site it where you can admire its color and fragrance up close, too. Held in large clusters, its red-blushed buds open into cupped to nearly flat semidouble ruffled flowers. Every blossom is different, with each petal streaked and flecked with varying amounts of red and white. They bloom most heavily in early summer, continuing with smaller flushes through the rest of the growing season, over large, somewhat glossy foliage on strong, thorny stems.

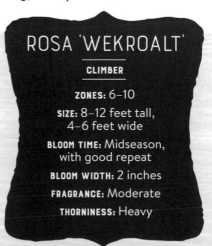

ROSA 'WEKROALT'

CLIMBER

ZONES: 6–10

SIZE: 8–12 feet tall, 4–6 feet wide

BLOOM TIME: Midseason, with good repeat

BLOOM WIDTH: 2 inches

FRAGRANCE: Moderate

THORNINESS: Heavy

how to use

Enjoy Fourth of July as a climber trained on an arbor or against a wall or fence. To create even more of a spectacle, combine it with another flowering climber, such as a morning glory (*Ipomoea* spp.). It looks particularly patriotic paired with a large-flowered hybrid clematis (*Clematis* hybrid) in the blue-purple range.

NEW DAWN

how to grow

'New Dawn' is a large-flowered climber that thrives in full sun in areas sheltered from winds. Set plants near a strong trellis or fence to give the vigorous canes adequate support. Amend the soil with organic matter and work it in well. For the first 2 to 3 years only, remove dead or damaged canes as needed. Afterward, you may improve the plant's profile and quality of bloom by taking out a couple of the older stems and trimming back the lateral stems. 'New Dawn' is not seriously troubled by pests or diseases, although slugs and aphids sometimes appear on the foliage. To control aphids, apply insecticidal soap; repeat as needed. Trap slugs by sinking margarine tubs into the ground and filling with beer.

Introduced in 1930, 'New Dawn' is a deservedly popular large-flowered climber. It bears quantities of soft, shell pink flowers during the growing season; they have high centers when they first open, but as they age, the loosely double flowers open to reveal gold stamens. When fully open, the blossoms have thirty-five petals and emit a sweet rose fragrance. 'New Dawn' grows upright and rampant, reaching 15 feet tall and up to 8 feet wide. Disease resistant and winter hardy, it has moderately thorny canes and shiny, medium green leaves.

ROSA 'NEW DAWN'
CLIMBER

ZONES: 5–9
SIZE: 12–15 feet tall, 8 feet wide
BLOOM TIME: Midseason, with good repeat
BLOOM WIDTH: 3 inches
FRAGRANCE: Moderate
THORNINESS: Moderate

how to use

'New Dawn' has many uses. Because of its rampant growth, you can use it as a tall ground cover or train it on a wall, pillar, or sturdy trellis. It makes an excellent hedge or, massed in the landscape, a superb focal point. 'New Dawn' produces flowers suitable for cutting.

WILLIAM BAFFIN

how to grow

'William Baffin' needs full sun and does best in well-worked soil to which some organic matter has been added. Fertilize after pruning in spring and in early summer. When grown as a climber, train the canes to a lateral support such as a rail fence for best flowering. When grown as a free-flowing shrub, allow the canes to arch to the ground for the heaviest flowering.

'William Baffin', one of the hardiest modern roses, is really two kinds of rose in one. You can grow this rose, known for vigor and disease resistance, as a dense, upright, somewhat arching shrub, or you can train it as a climber. It bears semidouble, twenty-petaled flowers in deep pink that grow in clusters of up to thirty. When fully open, the blossoms display vivid yellow stamens. The first flush of bloom occurs in midseason, and flowering repeats fairly well through early fall. Deadhead spent flowers to encourage continued flowering. While 'William Baffin' is not a prolific bloomer, it is hardy to temperatures down to −40°F and is pest- and disease-free. In particular, it is fully resistant to black spot, mildew, and rust—a plus in humid climates. Glossy, bright green leaves cover the long canes. Introduced in 1983 and named after a Canadian explorer, 'William Baffin' was developed at the Canadian Department of Agriculture's Central Experimental Farm in Ottawa, Ontario. Like other roses in the Explorer series, 'William Baffin' is ideal for gardens in the coldest climates.

how to use

'William Baffin' is perfect for gardens with cold winters and humid summers. Because of its upright habit and long bloom period, it works well as a tall hedge. It also makes an excellent climber if its tough canes are trained to a trellis or fence.

ROSA 'WILLIAM BAFFIN'

SHRUB

ZONES: 3–9

SIZE: 8–12 feet tall, 6 feet wide

BLOOM TIME: Midseason, excellent repeat

BLOOM WIDTH: 3–4 inches

FRAGRANCE: None

THORNINESS: Moderate

YELLOW LADY BANKS' ROSE

how to grow

While yellow Lady Banks' rose can tolerate light shade, it puts on its best show and most vigorous growth in rich soil that's on the average to moist side (but not soggy). It benefits from a generous layer of composted manure, garden compost, or chopped leaves applied as a mulch each year. It flowers on the previous year's growth, so hold off on pruning until it is finished flowering; then cut out any dead or damaged growth and trim the rest as needed to shape the plant and direct the growth where you want it to grow. This rambler might be affected by black spot, powdery mildew, or other roses diseases but generally not so much that it requires spraying.

Yellow Lady Banks' rose flowers only once a year, but what a glorious show it creates! This large, rambling rose is practically smothered with a glorious abundance of bloom in spring, well before other garden roses: bountiful clusters of small, double, buttery yellow blossoms that may be lightly scented. Best suited for warm-climate gardens, yellow Lady Banks' rose produces long, slender, gracefully arching canes that bear few thorns, if any. The rich green leaves have slender leaflets and are evergreen in most areas, possibly dropping in winter in the cooler parts of its growing range.

how to use

Plan on giving this vigorous rose plenty of space! Use it to cover a large arbor or pergola, or train it against a house wall or over a garden shed or other freestanding outbuilding. If you have a large property, consider letting yellow Lady Banks' rose grow unsupported as a large shrub, or let it ramble over a sloping site. To add a second season of interest, pair it with a clematis or another vine.

ROSA 'BANKSIAE LUTEA'

CLIMBER

ZONES: 7–10

SIZE: 15–20 feet tall,
6–10 feet wide

BLOOM TIME: Early season

BLOOM WIDTH: ¾ inch

FRAGRANCE: Light to none

THORNINESS: None

BURGUNDY ICEBERG

how to grow

In areas with hot summer or particularly intense sunshine, a bit of shade can help to maintain a deeper purple color on the blooms of Burgundy Iceberg. Elsewhere, give it full sun in a spot with enriched, well-drained soil. Apply a 1- to 2-inch-thick layer of an organic mulch, such as compost, to maintain soil fertility and moisture and suppress weeds. In late spring to early summer, trim out any dead, damaged, or crossing stems, then prune the remaining canes down to 12 to 19 inches. The plant generally shows good resistance to powdery mildew and rust but may be bothered by black spot. If you notice symptoms developing, pick off any affected leaves and spray the rest with a mixture of baking soda and water to discourage further disease development.

If you ask ten gardeners who grow Burgundy Iceberg to describe its color, you're likely to get ten different answers. In cool, cloudy weather, the petals can be a purple so deep it appears nearly black. In hot-summer areas, it's more of a pinkish purple—even magenta in intense sun. It may even show touches of cream to white in the very center or on the backs of the petals. Whatever the color, it's a pretty rose, with clusters of tapered, pointed buds that open to a cupped to somewhat flat form over medium green, somewhat glossy leaves. The plant has an overall rounded, bushy form.

how to use

Burgundy Iceberg makes an interesting addition to a cottage garden or a mixed border. The intriguing color of its blooms pairs well with whites and pinks, like those of summer phlox (*Phlox paniculata*) and purple coneflowers (*Echinacea purpurea*), as well as with a range of yellows— from chartreuse lady's mantle (*Alchemilla mollis*) to golden yellow coreopsis (*Coreopsis* spp.). Burgundy Iceberg also looks great planted in masses or as a naturally compact flowering hedge, by itself or paired with other Iceberg roses.

ROSA 'PROSE'

FLORIBUNDA

ZONES: 5–10

SIZE: 3–5 feet tall, 3–4 feet wide

BLOOM TIME: All season

BLOOM WIDTH: 3–4 inches

FRAGRANCE: Light

THORNINESS: Moderate to high

EASY TO PLEASE

how to grow

Easy to Please can tolerate a range of growing conditions, but to get the best show of blooms and healthiest growth, choose a planting site that provides full sun and average to moist but well-drained soil. Spread a 1- to 2-inch-thick layer of composted manure, chopped leaves, or other organic mulch around the base of the plant each year to maintain soil fertility, retain moisture, and keep weeds to a minimum. In late winter to early spring, cut out any dead or damaged canes, and any that are crossing; then prune the rest back to 12 to 18 inches to encourage good branching and bountiful flower production. Easy to Please generally shows good resistance to common rose diseases.

Part of the Easy to Love series, this well-named floribunda rose is a breeze to grow and filled with flowers. The clustered, pointed-oval buds produce a prolific display of large double flowers that have a cupped form and moderate, spicy scent. The petals are hot pink in cool weather, softening to medium pink in summer heat, with lighter pink undersides. When the blooms are fully open, they reveal a white eye zone around a cluster of bright yellow stamens. Easy to Please produces upright, moderately spreading plants with shiny, medium green foliage.

ROSA
'WEKFAWIBYBLU'

FLORIBUNDA

ZONES: 5–10
SIZE: 5–6 feet tall, 3–4 feet wide
BLOOM TIME: Midseason, with excellent repeat
BLOOM WIDTH: 2–3 inches
FRAGRANCE: Moderate
THORNINESS: Moderate

how to use

There are many ways to enjoy this easy-care rose in your yard. Enjoy it by itself in masses or as an informal flowering hedge, or combine it with other summer-flowering shrubs, such as hydrangeas (*Hydrangea* spp.). Easy to Please also works well in a mixed border with annuals and perennials, particularly those that bloom in white, yellow, purple, blue, or shades of pink. You can even try it in a large pot for a long season of color on a deck or patio.

EUROPEANA

how to grow

'Europeana' prefers locations with full sun but grows and flowers well in spots that receive 1 or 2 hours of light shade. Set plants in well-drained soil to which organic matter has been added. To promote heavy flowering, prune while dormant, cutting back the stems by two-thirds. 'Europeana' requires winter protection in Zone 5. It has some resistance to diseases but shows signs of black spot in summer and early fall. To control, apply fungicidal soap in spring when leaves begin to emerge; repeat as needed throughout summer. If insects such as aphids appear, apply insecticidal soap as needed.

This vigorous and bushy plant produces deep crimson, show-quality blooms. The flowers are cupped and semidouble with fifteen to twenty petals and a light tea fragrance. They bloom profusely in big clusters in midseason and repeat reliably thereafter. 'Europeana' has a rounded habit with bronze to reddish new foliage that ages to dark green. Its canes are moderately thorny. It performs best in areas with hot summers. Considered the best of all red floribundas, 'Europeana' was an All-America Rose Selection in 1968.

how to use

'Europeana' makes a wonderful bedding rose. To draw attention to its blooms, surround it with annuals and perennials (or other short roses) that bloom in pastel shades of yellow, cream, or peach. Foliage plants with silver leaves also act as a good foil. When 'Europeana' is planted en masse or as a hedge, the contrast between its dark red flowers and dark green leaves creates garden drama.

ROSA 'EUROPEANA'

FLORIBUNDA

ZONES: 5–9

SIZE: 2½–3 feet tall, 2 feet wide

BLOOM TIME: Midseason, with good repeat

BLOOM WIDTH: 3 inches

FRAGRANCE: Slight

THORNINESS: Moderate

HONEY PERFUME

how to grow

Full sun and average to moist but well-drained soil that has been enriched with compost is ideal. Encourage good root growth with a 1- to 2-inch-deep layer of an organic mulch, such as chopped leaves or composted manure, applied each year. To promote branching growth, which leads to best flowering, prune the plant in late winter or early spring. First, cut out any dead, damaged, or crossing stems; then snip the rest back by one-third to one-half, to a final height in the range of 12 to 18 inches. Honey Perfume typically shows good disease resistance but may be bothered by black spot in some areas. If you see dark discolorations on the foliage, pick off and discard affected leaves and spray those that are left with a mixture of baking soda and water to discourage further disease development.

The spicy scent of Honey Perfume earns it a place on many "most fragrant roses" lists. Held in clusters, its coral-brushed buds open to cupped, fully double flowers that typically start out as deep yellow, aging to cream or near white. In some conditions—particularly cool or cloudy weather—the petals develop a pinkish blush, giving the flowers an overall peachy or even orange appearance. The abundant blooms appear through most of the growing season over large, medium green leaves held on well-branched stems. The flowers tend to be largest and last the longest during the first flush of bloom, then again in fall.

ROSA 'JACARQUE'
FLORIBUNDA
ZONES: 6–9
SIZE: 3–4 feet tall, 2–3 feet wide
BLOOM TIME: Midseason, with excellent repeat
BLOOM WIDTH: 4 inches
FRAGRANCE: Moderate to strong
THORNINESS: Moderate

how to use

Plant Honey Perfume in masses as a landscape accent or as a flowering low hedge. It also looks lovely in a cottage garden or a mixed border. If possible, site it near a sitting area or use it in a foundation planting, so you can enjoy the fragrance up close or through an open window. Its peachy to yellow blooms are stunning against a backdrop of deep purple foliage, like that of 'Royal Purple' smoke bush (*Cotinus coggygria*).

ICEBERG

how to grow

Iceberg thrives in a sunny location in soil that is fertile and well drained. For best flower production, prune plants when dormant, cutting canes back by two-thirds. Fertilize with a complete rose fertilizer after pruning and again after the first flowers have faded. Deadhead spent flowers to encourage continual bloom. This beautiful rose is vulnerable to diseases such as black spot and powdery mildew, so give it extra protection to keep it looking its best. Aphids and Japanese beetles can become bothersome in summer. To control, apply an insecticidal soap as needed.

Renowned for the beauty of its pristine white flowers, Iceberg starts blooming in early to midseason and continues all season long. It is floriferous, producing abundant clusters of fragrant flowers with thirty petals. The hybrid-tea-shaped flowers open to a cupped shape, revealing a central tuft of showy gold stamens. This tough, hardy floribunda is also extremely disease resistant—except to black spot—and vigorous. It has upright, bushy growth and semi-glossy, light green leaves. Iceberg won a Royal National Rose Society Gold Medal in 1958.

how to use

Iceberg makes an impressive hedge and is well suited to mass plantings.

ROSA 'KORBIN'

FLORIBUNDA

ZONES: 5–9

SIZE: 4 feet tall

BLOOM TIME: Early to midseason, with all-season repeat

BLOOM WIDTH: 3 inches

FRAGRANCE: Moderate

THORNINESS: Moderate

JULIA CHILD

how to grow

For optimal flowering and most vigorous growth, give this rose a planting site with plenty of sun and fertile soil that's moist but well drained. It's also a good idea to provide a yearly application of an organic mulch, such as garden compost, in a 1- to 2-inch-thick layer around the base of the plant each year. Prune it in late winter to early spring, first removing any dead, broken, or crossing stems; then cut the remaining stems back by one-third to one-half, to leave a final height of 12 to 18 inches. Julia Child generally shows above-average disease resistance but may be susceptible to black spot in humid conditions. Spraying with a mixture of baking soda and water can help to discourage the development of this fungal disease.

Yellow roses hold a special place in the hearts of many gardeners, and this one is a winner among these beauties. Julia Child offers an abundance of plump, clustered buds that open to display fully double, cupped to ruffled flowers. Packed with petals, the blooms may appear almost peachy yellow at first, quickly turning to a bright, clear yellow. They often age to a softer buttery to creamy yellow, especially in hot conditions and strong sun, giving an almost multicolored appearance. The scent, which is usually described as licorice-like, tends to be quite noticeable. Julia Child bears glossy, medium green leaves and has a compact, bushy growth habit.

ROSA 'WEKVOSSUTONO'

FLORIBUNDA

ZONES: 5–10

SIZE: About 3 feet tall, 3–4 feet wide

BLOOM TIME: Midseason, with good repeat

BLOOM WIDTH: 3–4 inches

FRAGRANCE: Moderate to strong

THORNINESS: Heavy

how to use

Use Julia Child to line a path or walkway, or tuck it into a flower bed or cottage garden. Its compact size also makes it a good choice for container growing. Complement the yellow flowers with companions that have white flowers, such as Shasta daisy (*Leucanthemum* x *superbum*), or with rosy pinks, like those of red valerian (*Centranthus ruber*) or purple coneflower (*Echinacea purpurea*). It also pairs perfectly with purples and blues.

LOVE

how to grow

Love isn't too particular, as roses go, but will give you its best flowering and healthiest growth in an ideal site: one with plenty of sun and fertile, moist but well-drained soil. A 1- to 2-inch-deep layer of organic mulch—chopped leaves or composted manure, for example—spread around the base of the plant each spring will provide optimal conditions for the roots and help to discourage weeds as well. The yearly pruning is simply a matter of removing any dead, damaged, or spindly stems and then trimming the rest down to 12 to 18 inches to encourage bushy new growth. Love is rarely bothered by powdery mildew but may develop a bit of black spot in some climates. Use preventive sprays (such as baking soda mixed with water) to discourage the disease if it is common in your area.

A time-tested selection enjoyed by gardeners across the country, Love is distinctive for its two-toned flowers. Tapered buds open into high-centered blooms that closely resemble those of a classic hybrid tea rose. The upper side of each petal is a velvety red to cerise color—often turning more of a magenta-pink hue in summer—with a strongly contrasting white underside, giving the blooms a bicolor appearance when you see them from the side. They may appear singly or in clusters over the glossy, deep green leaves. Love is generally described as scentless, but some gardeners claim to detect a good fragrance. If that trait is important to you, look for plants sold in bloom and sniff before you buy.

how to use

Grow Love by itself in a grouping or as an informal hedge, or combine it with annual and perennial companions and other shrubs in a mixed border. In the garden or as a cut flower, it's particularly pretty with partners that have white flowers or white-variegated foliage, which will echo the white underside of the rose's petals.

ROSA 'JACTWIN'

GRANDIFLORA

ZONES: 5–10
SIZE: 3–5 feet tall, 2–4 feet wide
BLOOM TIME: All season
BLOOM WIDTH: 3–4 inches
FRAGRANCE: Slight to none
THORNINESS: Heavy

MISTER LINCOLN

how to grow

One of the more beautiful hybrid tea roses, 'Mister Lincoln' needs extra attention to stay healthy and look its best. Plant in an open, lightly breezy area in full sun. Amend the soil with lots of organic matter. Prune when dormant, cutting back all canes by two-thirds and removing any thin or diseased stems. Fertilize in spring after pruning and again when the first blossoms fade. Apply a fungicidal soap or garden sulfur in spring and repeat applications as needed throughout the growing season. If pests such as aphids appear, treat with insecticidal soap.

'Mister Lincoln' produces large flowers of dark velvety red that start as pointed buds. As the flowers mature, they exhibit a classic, high-centered shape and then develop a cupped form filled with thirty to forty petals. They exude a vibrant damask rose scent. Set against rich, leathery, dark green leaves, the flowers dazzle with their outstanding beauty and powerful scent. An All-America Rose Selection for 1965, 'Mister Lincoln' has an upright, well-branched form. It is disease resistant and winter hardy.

ROSA 'MISTER LINCOLN'

HYBRID TEA

ZONES: 5–9
SIZE: 4–5 feet tall, 2–3 feet wide
BLOOM TIME: All season
BLOOM WIDTH: 5 inches
FRAGRANCE: Strong
THORNINESS: Moderate

how to use

Use 'Mister Lincoln' in massed plantings or as a hedge. The bush's form is a bit stiff for any but the most formal flower gardens; it looks better in the company of other hybrid tea roses. Because of its long stems and glorious blooms, it makes an excellent cut flower. Plant enough so you can cut several blooms without ruining the display.

OLYMPIAD

how to grow

Olympiad is a remarkably sturdy rose, often adapting to less-than-ideal growing conditions. To get the most bountiful display of beautiful blooms, though, give it plenty of sun and a spot with fertile, moist but well-drained soil. Spread a 1- to 2-inch-deep layer of composted manure or other organic mulch around it each year to provide ideal conditions for good root growth. Pruning is simple: First, cut out any dead or damaged canes in late winter or early spring. Then remove any spindly stems (those thinner than a pencil). Trim the remaining stems down to about 6 inches, making your cuts just above an outward-facing bud. Olympiad generally shows good resistance to common rose diseases but may be bothered by black spot. If this fungal disease is common in your area, consider using sprays of baking soda mixed with water to discourage it from developing.

If a classic red rose is on your gardening wish list, Olympiad belongs at the top of your must-trys. Its high-centered blooms are practically perfect in form, with thick rich red petals that hold their vibrant color remarkably well in hot climates. Usually held singly atop long stems, the fully double flowers appear abundantly throughout the growing season over somewhat glossy, medium to light green leaves. Perhaps the only improvement one could wish for would be a stronger scent: the fragrance is generally on the light side. Olympiad plants are vigorous, bushy, and upright.

how to use

Let Olympiad be a star planted by itself in groups as a landscape accent, or add it to flower beds, borders, or foundation plantings. It is also an excellent choice for a cutting garden, producing an abundance of long-lasting, long-stemmed blooms for arrangements. In the garden or in a bouquet, it looks equally lovely paired with whites and silvers; combined with bright oranges, yellows, and purples; or set among shades of clear pink.

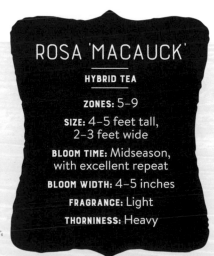

ROSA 'MACAUCK'

HYBRID TEA

ZONES: 5–9

SIZE: 4–5 feet tall, 2–3 feet wide

BLOOM TIME: Midseason, with excellent repeat

BLOOM WIDTH: 4–5 inches

FRAGRANCE: Light

THORNINESS: Heavy

PEACE

how to grow

'Peace' prefers at least 6 hours of sun per day but can tolerate a bit of shade. It flowers best in moist, ordinary to fertile soil with good drainage and grows best east of the Rocky Mountains. Prune in late winter or early spring when plants are dormant; remove any dead and diseased canes and lightly cut back remaining stems. Fertilize with a complete rose fertilizer after pruning. To control black spot and mildew, spray the young leaves with fungicidal soap, repeating every few weeks throughout the growing season. Control insects by applying insecticidal soap as needed. In Zone 5, plants need winter protection to prevent damage.

Possibly the most widely known of all roses, 'Peace' produces large yellow flowers edged in pink. The big blooms are double, with forty to forty-five petals and a faint, fruity scent. The flowers exhibit a classic high-centered hybrid tea shape. When fully open, the blossom may reveal a divided center, but overall its mature shape is large, full, and pleasing. Disease resistant and winter hardy, 'Peace' has large, shiny dark green foliage and somewhat thorny canes. It has won awards throughout North America and Europe, including a designation as an All-America Rose Selection in 1946.

ROSA 'PEACE'

HYBRID TEA

ZONES: 5–9
SIZE: 5–6 feet tall, 2½ feet wide
BLOOM TIME: All season
BLOOM WIDTH: 6 inches
FRAGRANCE: Slight to none
THORNINESS: Moderate

how to use

Use 'Peace' as a specimen, since on its own it can make an impressive sight. Although most hybrid teas look better when planted close together because of their upright, narrow, or sometimes scraggly habits, 'Peace' is a full enough shrub to be planted on its own. Its blooms make excellent cut flowers.

QUEEN ELIZABETH

how to grow

Plant 'Queen Elizabeth' in a location with full sun in well-drained soil that has been amended with plenty of organic matter. In late winter or early spring while plants are dormant, remove dead and damaged canes. Cut back remaining stems by one-half to three-quarters to promote the best flowering and vigorous growth. Fertilize with a balanced rose fertilizer after pruning and again after the first flowers fade. Remove spent blooms to encourage the production of more flowers and reduce the spread of diseases. In Zone 5, mound loose soil around the graft in fall after the ground has frozen. 'Queen Elizabeth' often shows signs of black spot and mildew in summer. To control, apply a fungicidal soap in early spring and repeat as needed. Control insects such as aphids with insecticidal soap.

The first, best, and by far most popular grandiflora, 'Queen Elizabeth' produces substantial pink flowers with up to forty petals each. The large, double pink blossoms have a high-centered to cupped form and a moderate tea fragrance, and they bloom constantly. They appear singly and in small, long-stemmed clusters. Disease-resistant 'Queen Elizabeth' has shiny, leathery dark green leaves and somewhat thorny canes. It has won awards throughout North America and Europe, including a designation as an All-America Rose Selection in 1955.

how to use

With its long stems and large, beautiful blossoms, 'Queen Elizabeth' makes a fabulous cut flower. Because of its tall stature, you can plant it behind shorter shrubs or roses for a fuller look, or use it on its own in hedges or bold massed plantings.

ROSA 'QUEEN ELIZABETH'

GRANDIFLORA

ZONES: 5–9

SIZE: 5–7 feet tall, 2½–3 feet wide

BLOOM TIME: Midseason, with excellent repeat

BLOOM WIDTH: 4 inches

FRAGRANCE: Moderate

THORNINESS: Moderate

TOUCH OF CLASS

how to grow

Touch of Class does best in a sunny, lightly breezy location in soil that is well drained and amended with lots of organic matter. Prune in spring when plants are dormant, cutting back all canes by two-thirds and removing any thin stems. Deadhead spent flowers to encourage heavy bloom. Fertilize with a balanced fertilizer (see page 119). To control diseases, particularly mildew, apply garden sulfur or fungicidal soap in spring and repeat as needed throughout the season. If insects such as aphids become a problem, apply an insecticidal soap.

A popular exhibition rose, Touch of Class produces large coral-pink blooms shaded orange and cream with a perfect high-centered hybrid tea form. The large blooms are double, with thirty-three petals and a soft tea fragrance. Disease resistant and winter hardy, Touch of Class has shiny dark green foliage and somewhat thorny canes. New growth is a mahogany, enhancing the richness of the coral-pink blooms, which keep their pinpoint centers as the buds unfurl. Touch of Class has an erect, bushy habit. It was an All-America Rose Selection in 1984.

ROSA 'KRICARLO'

HYBRID TEA

ZONES: 5–9
SIZE: 4–5 feet tall, 3 feet wide
BLOOM TIME: All season
BLOOM WIDTH: 5 inches
FRAGRANCE: Slight to none
THORNINESS: Moderate

how to use

The long stems on Touch of Class, its uniquely colorful petals, and its perfect form make it an ideal cut flower. Grow it in a rose bed with other hybrid teas and floribundas, where it will be an impressive sight.

TROPICANA

how to grow

Tropicana prefers at least 6 hours of sun per day but will tolerate a little shade. It flowers best in moist, fertile soil with good drainage. Prune in spring before new growth begins, cutting back all canes by two-thirds and removing any thin, spindly growth. To control black spot, powdery mildew, and other diseases, apply a fungicidal soap or garden sulfur to new leaves in spring and repeat monthly throughout the growing season. If pests such as aphids appear, apply an insecticidal soap as needed. Tropicana is more prone to mildew when grown in dry regions of the western states.

Vivid orange color and classic form make Tropicana a superstar among roses. Actually, this rose is known as Super Star in Europe, where it was introduced in 1960. It produces large blooms with thirty to thirty-five petals and a classic high-centered hybrid tea form. The blossoms have a sweet, fruity scent and bloom plentifully. Tropicana has large pointed buds and fairly shiny, dark green foliage on long, rather thorny stems. It has an erect, well-branched, bushy habit. It was an All-America Rose Selection in 1963.

how to use

Tropicana looks striking massed in a rose bed. It is an attractive cut flower; you may wish to grow an extra bush in an out-of-the-way location so you can cut often for arrangements without diminishing the display.

ROSA
'TANORSTAR'

HYBRID TEA

ZONES: 5–9

SIZE: 4–5 feet tall,
3 feet wide

BLOOM TIME: All season

BLOOM WIDTH: 5 inches

FRAGRANCE: Moderate

THORNINESS: Moderate
to very

ALL A'TWITTER

how to grow

The ideal growing site for All a'Twitter has full sun and well-drained soil. It can tolerate light shade but may flower less there. If rainfall is lacking, water as needed to keep the soil evenly moist. Add a 1- to 2-inch layer of compost or other organic mulch around the plant in spring to help maintain soil fertility and moisture. Prune the plant in late winter or early spring to remove any dead or damaged stems, maintain the overall shape, and encourage branching growth. All a'Twitter is naturally vigorous and has very good disease resistance, so it seldom needs spraying.

If you're looking for a bright splash of color for your garden, All a'Twitter is an excellent choice. In cool conditions, the semidouble flowers are a rich orange color; in hot weather, they're a bit more on the salmon-orange side. The open blooms are cupped in form, opening to reveal a bright yellow center, and may form singly or in small clusters. New flowers continue to appear through the growing season, showing off beautifully against glossy deep green foliage. All a'Twitter (also sold as All A Twitter) produces bushy, upright plants.

ROSA 'WEKCOFBUNK'

MINIATURE

ZONES: 4–10

SIZE: 18–36 inches tall, 12–18 inches wide

BLOOM TIME: All season

BLOOM WIDTH: 2 inches

FRAGRANCE: Very light

THORNINESS: Moderate

how to use

The compact size of All a'Twitter means it fits easily into smaller gardens. Enjoy it in flower beds or borders, in groups on its own or combined with other plants. It also works well in large containers on a deck or patio. For a traffic-stopping show, pair it with bright yellow companions, such as annual 'Profusion Yellow' zinnia (*Zinnia* hybrid) or perennial coreopsis (*Coreopsis* spp.). Or let the rose flowers be the star by pairing them with deep purple foliage partners, such as annual 'Red Rubin' basil (*Ocimum basilicum*) or perennial 'Plum Pudding' alumroot (*Heuchera* hybrid). The orange flowers also pair beautifully with blue- or purple-flowered partners.

ROSA 'WEKWIBYPUR'

MINIATURE

ZONES: 5–9

SIZE: 18–36 inches tall,
24–36 inches wide

BLOOM TIME: All season

BLOOM WIDTH: 2 inches

FRAGRANCE: Moderate to strong

THORNINESS: Moderate

DIAMOND EYES

how to grow

Diamond Eyes thrives in a site with full sun and enriched, well-drained soil. Apply a 1- to 2-inch-deep layer of organic much, such as chopped leaves, around the plant each spring to help retain soil moisture, maintain soil fertility, and suppress weeds. Water during dry spells to keep the soil moist. Prune in late winter or early spring to encourage dense, bushy growth and many flowers. Diamond Eyes generally has good disease resistance, but black spot may be a problem in some areas. If you notice symptoms developing, pick off the affected leaves and spray the rest with a solution of baking soda and water to discourage further development of the disease.

Do you want fragrance? Do you want knock-your-socks-off color? You want to grow Diamond Eyes! This distinctive miniature rose produces an abundance of flowers through the growing season, though sometimes taking a short break through the worst of summer's heat. In spring and fall, particularly, the velvety petals are so deep burgundy that they can almost appear black; in summer, they are a deep pinkish purple. As the cupped, double blooms open to be nearly flat, they reveal a white eye and golden yellow center, and they release a rich, spicy scent: a trait not often found among miniature roses. The flowers are held in small clusters over glossy medium green leaves on bushy, upright plants.

how to use

Grow Diamond Eyes in a flower bed or border, or in a large container on your deck, by a pool, or next to your favorite garden bench: anywhere you can get close to enjoy its delightful fragrance. The unusual color and spicy scent also make the blooms lovely as cut flowers for small arrangements. Choose companions with white flowers or white-variegated leaves to contrast with the main petal color and repeat the white eye of the flowers. Silver foliage, like that of dusty miller (*Senecio cineraria*) or wormwoods

GOURMET POPCORN

how to grow

Gourmet Popcorn is a tough, adaptable rose. It thrives in full sun and moist, fertile soil but can also perform surprisingly well in less-than-ideal conditions, such as light shade (particularly in hot climates). Treat the plants to an organic mulch, such as chopped leaves or compost, to encourage good root growth and suppress weeds. Apply it 1 to 2 inches deep around the base of the plant in spring. The plants flower on new growth, so prune accordingly in early spring. Remove any dead, damaged, or crossing stems, then trim the rest back by one-third to one-half. Gourmet Popcorn is seldom bothered by common rose diseases.

When you see the abundant, rounded buds explode into an abundance of brilliant white blooms, you'll know how Gourmet Popcorn got its name. The deep green, somewhat shiny leaves are nearly smothered by the clustered, semidouble blooms, which open cupped to nearly flat to reveal small yellow centers. The flowers have a pleasant sweet scent and appear through most of the growing season, giving you a big show in a relatively small space. Gourmet Popcorn plants have a rounded, bushy shape.

ROSA 'WEOPOP'

MINIATURE ROSE

ZONES: 5–10

SIZE: 18–30 inches tall, 2–3 feet wide

BLOOM TIME: All season

BLOOM WIDTH: 1 inch

FRAGRANCE: Moderate

THORNINESS: Light to moderate

how to use

There are endless ways to enjoy this versatile rose. Grow it alone as a specimen in a small garden, add it to a mixed planting in a bed or border, or grow it in masses as a ground cover. It also looks spectacular cascading out of a large container or even a big hanging basket. Its crisp white blooms combine nicely with any companion color, holding up well with equally bright colors and adding sparkle to pastel plantings. It's also invaluable for providing a long season of interest in a white garden, paired with other white flowers and white-variegated or silvery foliage partners.

ROSA 'SAVALIFE'

MINIATURE

ZONES: 5–9

SIZE: 1–2 feet tall,
1–2 feet wide

BLOOM TIME: All season

BLOOM WIDTH: 1–2 inches

FRAGRANCE: Light

THORNINESS: Moderate

RAINBOW'S END

how to grow

Rainbow's End performs surprisingly well in some shade, but ample sun brings out the most intense colors on the flowers. Average, well-drained soil is fine. Keep the soil around the base of the plant covered with a 1- to 2-inch-thick layer of chopped leaves, garden compost, or another organic mulch to provide ideal conditions for vigorous root growth and suppress weeds. Prune in late winter to early spring, first removing any dead or damaged stems; then trim the remaining canes back by one-third to one-half to encourage bushy new growth and lots of flowers. Rainbow's End typically shows good resistance to common rose diseases but may develop black spot in humid areas, so consider using preventive sprays of baking soda mixed with water.

Rainbow's End rose is classified as a miniature, but it makes a big presence wherever it grows. The clustered, golden to red-blushed buds open into fully double flowers that look like perfectly scaled-down hybrid tea rose blossoms. The newly opened blooms are yellow, quickly becoming blushed with hot pink to red on the edges (the stronger the sun they're exposed to, the richer the colors). They eventually age to mostly pink and white. The flowers last for quite a while, so there are blooms of many different ages (and colors) on the plant at one time. Their scent tends to be light. The bushy plants produce proportionally small medium green leaves that are somewhat glossy.

how to use

With its bountiful display of multicolored blooms, Rainbow's End is a wonderful choice for brightening up small spaces. Enjoy it in a flower bed, in a foundation planting, or along a path or walkway. It looks terrific in a container, too, and is wonderful as a cut flower in small arrangements. In the garden or in bouquets, try pairing it with deep purple-blue flowers, like those of perennial salvias (*Salvia* spp.), or a dark-leaved alumroot (*Heuchera* hybrid), such as 'Plum Pudding'.

RUBY RUBY

how to grow

This lovely little rose gives its best performance in a spot with ample sun and compost-enriched, well-drained soil. Give it a 1- to 2-inch-thick layer of composted manure, chopped leaves, or other organic mulch to maintain soil fertility and promote healthy root growth. Water thoroughly during dry spells. Flowers appear on the new growth, so good pruning in late winter to early spring will give you the most abundant display. Clip out any dead or damaged canes first, then any that are rubbing against each other. Finish with removing some of the twiggy growth in the center of the plant and trimming back the remaining canes by one-third to one-half to shape the plant. During the growing season, clip off faded flowers to encourage rebloom. Ruby Ruby shows good resistance to common rose diseases in most areas, but if you notice discoloration on the foliage, pick off affected leaves and spray the remaining canes with a mixture of baking soda and water to discourage further damage.

Ruby Ruby offers a big presence in a small package. Held in small clusters, the tapered buds produce fully double flowers that open to a cupped and then nearly flat form. The petals are a rich shade of ruby-red, holding their color well over the life of the flower, even in hot summer weather. The lightly fragrant blossoms show off beautifully against the glossy dark green foliage, on plants that have a low, bushy to somewhat spreading habit.

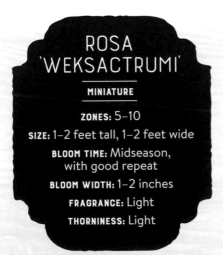

ROSA 'WEKSACTRUMI'

MINIATURE

ZONES: 5–10
SIZE: 1–2 feet tall, 1–2 feet wide
BLOOM TIME: Midseason, with good repeat
BLOOM WIDTH: 1–2 inches
FRAGRANCE: Light
THORNINESS: Light

how to use

Site Ruby Ruby near the front of a flower bed or mixed border, plant it along a path, or grow it in a pot on your patio or poolside: anywhere you can enjoy its charming flowers up close. The rich red color of this marvelous miniature positively glows in the garden, particularly when paired with companions that have bright white flowers or silvery foliage.

BEST TIPS

FOR GROWING ROSES, HERBS, AND EDIBLE FLOWERS

deadheading: precision counts

Pruning back fading flowers after a bush has bloomed is called "deadheading." This keeps your plant looking neat; also, it encourages more flowering and new growth. Otherwise, plants spend energy going to seed—that is, forming hips. Always use good, sharp pruners.

1. Find the first pair of five-leaflet leaves below the spent flower. If there are several pairs of three-leaflet leaves below it, play it safe and cut above the second pair instead. (If you want your older roses to have longer stems for bouquets, you may cut the stem at the second five-leaflet leaf.)

2. Cut about one-fourth inch above the targeted spot, at a 45-degree angle pointing away from the center of the plant. Be precise, because a cut that is made too high will result in weak, thin new growth that is likely to fail.

3. Stop deadheading a month before frost to help plants prepare for winter.

making a proper pruning cut

While cutting into a healthy rose branch may cause a moment of trepidation, the positive results will make any anxiety worthwhile.

1. Buy quality pruning shears, and keep them sharp. Inexpensive and dull ones crush or mash rather than slice.

2. Make your cut just above a healthy, outward-facing bud or a promising side branch. The goal is to inspire new growth that grows away from the center of the bush, not into it.

   Conventional wisdom counsels about one-fourth inch above, but do your best. If you cut too far from a bud, the result is a dead stub that may invite disease into the stem. If you cut too close to a bud, it can dry out or be damaged by freezing weather.

3. Always cut at a slant to the stem, at about a 45-degree angle. Such cuts dry out faster after a rain, and too much dampness encourages disease.

4. Ideally, the cut should slope downward toward the center of the bush.

fertilizing roses

Roses are greedy eaters but reward you with strong growth and plenty of flowers. Use a balanced or rose fertilizer and follow label directions for the correct amount.

1. At planting time, add slow-release fertilizer to the planting hole. Also feed when you prune each spring.

2. Beginning right after the first flush of blooms fades, feed new and established roses monthly during the growing season, stopping 6 to 8 weeks before frost.

3. Sprinkle fertilizer evenly around the plant at the "drip line" (the imaginary circle around the outer edge of the leaves). Scratch it in with a trowel or cultivator and water well.

rose hip jam

Rose hips have a vitamin C content that is four hundred times greater than that of oranges. So they are a popular and practical ingredient in jams and jellies; the sweet-tart taste and aroma and pretty rose color are pluses.

TO MAKE ROSE HIP JAM

4 cups rose hip puree

5 cups sugar

1 tablespoon lemon juice

1. Collect hips when they are firm and ripe or almost ripe, and gently wash them in clear, cool water.

2. Prepare a puree by adding just enough water to cover the hips. Simmer until the hips are soft. Put the pulp through a food mill.

3. Combine the pulp, sugar, and lemon juice. Bring the mixture to a boil, then reduce heat. Simmer until thickened and desired consistency is reached.

4. Ladle jam into hot sterilized jars and seal.

MAKES TWO TO THREE PINTS

transplanting a rose

If a rose doesn't look quite as attractive as you thought it would in a particular spot, or if it outgrows its location, transplanting is in order. This does not have to be a traumatic experience for the plant. Just make sure you undertake the operation at the best time—while the rose is still dormant in early spring or late winter.

1. Water the soil deeply the day before transplanting.

2. Prepare an ample hole in the new location (18 inches wide and deep, or more), with soil and amendments to one side so you'll be ready to backfill.

3. With a shovel or spade, dig a hole around the plant at least 18 inches in diameter—wider if it is particularly large.

4. Gently remove the plant with its soil ball intact. Take care not to disturb the roots.

5. Place the rose in its new location. Always replant at the same depth as it grew previously (there will be a soil line visible low down on the main stem or stems).

6. Cut the top growth back by one-third to one-half. This reduces stress on the root system so it can devote itself instead to establishing the plant in the new spot.

BEST
TIPS

a short course on soil ph

Testing your soil is one way to make sure that you are providing the best growing conditions for your plants to thrive.

You can test the relative acidity or alkalinity of your soil with a soil-testing kit, available from most nurseries and garden centers. Or you can send soil samples to your local extension service, often located at a university.

Neutral pH is 7. Any number below that is acidic; above is alkaline. Most plants do well in slightly acidic to neutral soil with a pH of 6 to 7.

To render soil more alkaline, add lime to it according to the results of the soil test. Soil in the hot, dry climate of the Southwest tends to be alkaline, while soil in forested areas of the Northeast and Northwest is often acidic.

making plants bushier

After your plant has reached 6 inches high, pinch back the growing tip at the top of the plant. When new shoots appear along the sides, use your thumb and index finger to pinch out the tips of the new side stems to encourage a more compact, bushier plant.

If you let the plant flower, pinch off dead blooms so the plant puts its energy into making more stems, flowers, and foliage instead of setting seeds.

nutrients: the big three

For a long, healthy life, roses must have nitrogen, phosphorus, and potassium. These elements occur naturally in the soil. If there is a deficiency, it's up to you to provide supplements. Your roses will richly reward your care with lusher, healthier growth and more blooms.

Nitrogen (N) is the most important element. Without the right amount, roses have a poor start in spring, stunted growth, weak stems, few flowers, and yellow leaves. Too much causes more leaves than flowers and soft growth that is more susceptible to disease and vulnerable to frost damage. Add nitrogen to the soil using compost or fish emulsion.

Phosphorus (P) encourages a healthy root system as well as more and larger flowers. Your rose is not getting enough if its leaves turn dark green on top and purple below. Many fertilizers contain high amounts of this element, or you can add it solo in the form of bonemeal or superphosphate.

Potassium (K) deficiency results in poor flower production or color, weak stems, and wilting or yellow tips. As with phosphorus, potassium can be added to the soil in fertilizer or with 1 tablespoon per plant of potassium nitrate in early summer.

BEST TIPS

gathering roots while growing flowers

For some plants, such as purple coneflower, the most potent medicinal part is not the flower but the root. Here's how to collect the roots without harvesting the entire plant.

1. To have both medicinal roots and beautiful flowers, allow plants to grow undisturbed until they form a thick clump, about 3 to 4 years.

2. In spring or fall, lift the clump from the ground with a garden fork and shake off excess soil.

3. Divide the clump with a sharp knife, leaving each division with plenty of roots.

4. Cut the longest root from each division and set aside so that the remaining roots are left intact. Replant the division in the desired location.

5. Wash the taproot; place in a warm, dark room until completely dry. Store in a dark-colored glass jar that is tightly sealed.

making candied herbs

Candy herb flowers for a garnish by lightly painting them with egg whites and then dipping them in very fine sugar. A mixture of 1 tablespoon of gum arabic and 1 tablespoon of warm water can be substituted for the raw egg whites if desired.

propagation by layering

Use this simple layering technique for propagating lavender and other woody herbs, such as rosemary and winter savory.

1. Strip the leaves from a flexible shoot but leave the foliage on the stem tip.

2. Nick the stem where you want the roots to grow.

3. Make a shallow trench and bend the stem to the ground. Peg it into the soil, using a hairpin-shaped wire, a rock, or a small mound of soil.

4. Water regularly. After the stem has developed its own root system, sever it from its parent and replant.

BEST TIPS

propagation from cuttings

Many herbs, from mint to scented geraniums (pictured above), can be easily propagated from transplanted stem cuttings.

1. Pinch a 4-inch-long stem just beneath a set of leaves. Cut the end with a sharp knife and remove the lowest set of leaves from the stem.

2. Fill a clean pot with moist potting mix and poke a 2-inch-deep hole in the soil.

3. Insert the cutting in the hole and gently firm the soil around the stem.

4. Keep in a warm spot in filtered light, and mist daily. Cuttings of most herbs will root in a month or two. Rooted cuttings can be overwintered as houseplants.

Some herbs, such as winter savory, lavender, sage, rosemary, and thyme, thrive in sandy soils and prefer to grow on dry hillsides where they are native.

1. Set transplants of these five plants on the dry slope, spacing them 18 inches apart.

2. Plant the herbs and mulch lightly with an inorganic mulch like washed gravel.

3. Water regularly until established. The plants will not only lend beauty to the hillside, but fill the surrounding air with their spicy aromas as well.

BEST TIPS

INTRODUCTION TO HERBS AND EDIBLE FLOWERS

Of the many types of plants that grow in our gardens, herbs hold a very special place. For centuries, we have studied them, grown them, and used them. Humanity, it seems, cultivated herbs even before it cultivated civilization. In short, herbs have been our partners for a very long time.

People have used herbs to heal their bodies, calm their minds, add fragrance to their homes, and flavor and preserve their foods. They have been used to stuff mattresses, repel pests, and attract butterflies and birds to soothe our spirits. Herbs improve the quality of our lives. In a world as fast-paced as ours, this is, indeed, a very special contribution.

herbs as magic

The value of herbs has never been questioned by the societies that used them. However, just how they accomplish their myriad wonders has been a mystery through the ages. For generations, science was not sophisticated enough to reveal the secrets of herbs. Lacking the scientific answers, people devised magical ones instead.

To the Egyptians, the onion was sacred; they believed that the layers of the bulb symbolized the different layers of the universe. Herbs were used to prepare the bodies of deceased pharaohs for their afterlife journey and to decorate their resting places. In ancient Greece, sweet bay was considered much more than a plant. This warm, spicy herb was regarded as the transformed nymph Daphne, who offered herself to the people as sweet bay to escape the unwanted advances of the god Apollo.

To other peoples, such as the Jews of the Middle East, herbs were considered medicines harvested from the earth by humans, but created and endowed with their curative powers by God.

finding answers

Today, modern science has replaced the magic and mystery of herbs with logic and reason. The compounds and chemicals responsible for the many attributes of herbs are slowly but surely coming to light. The burning spiciness of hot peppers, the relaxing aroma of lavender, the soothing quality of chamomile—these and many other qualities of herbs have come under close scrutiny. Not surprisingly, many of the folk remedies and ancient uses ascribed to herbs have been validated by modern science. Hot peppers are still used to relieve pain, as they have been for hundreds of years; lavender still helps people get a good night's sleep; and chamomile is a favorite home remedy for an upset stomach. Science has cast a different light on our partnership with herbs, an illumination that continues to validate the importance and versatility of these wonderful plants.

ALL THE BEST

This guide is a compendium of the most useful herbs commonly grown today—our best herb-garden partners. The plants are arranged alphabetically by scientific name, with the common name in large type just above the scientific one. Each plant is identified with a large photograph accompanied by an at-a-glance box with a brief list of important features, including plant hardiness, type and size, identifying characteristics, and the plant's principal uses. An introduction acquaints you with the herb's special attributes.

In "How to Grow" you'll find the necessary cultural techniques as well as the conditions required, such as the best type of soil, directions for watering, and maintenance techniques specific to the featured herb. The best method of propagation is also highlighted in this section—you'll know whether to sow seeds, take cuttings, or divide the plant to grow additional plants.

Following the growing information, you'll find the most common uses of the herb. Here the parts of the plant and their common uses are identified. Harvesting and storage techniques are included, along with methods of preparation.

At your fingertips, you have all the information you need to get started in herb gardening and to learn how to use and enjoy herbs all year long.

BEST HERBS AND EDIBLE FLOWERS

ANISE HYSSOP

how to grow

This pest-free herb is native to the North American prairies and thrives in average, well-drained soil in full sun to light shade. Too much shade or nitrogen fertilizer often produces a floppy plant that requires staking. Sow seeds or transplant self-sown seedlings in spring. Divide in fall from Zone 7 south, and spring elsewhere. To keep the plant from increasing too rapidly, snip off the blossoms before they can produce seeds.

Dense spikes of 3-inch-long violet blooms top the stiff upright stems of this neat, sweetly scented perennial. Anise hyssop stems have four sides, like other members of the mint family. Its common names—anise hyssop, blue giant hyssop, and fennel giant hyssop—derive from the plant's sweet licorice fragrance and similar appearance to hyssop, another member of the mint family. The soft, pointed leaves are flushed with purple in early spring and turn bright green by the time the plants are fully grown.

AGASTACHE FOENICULUM

ZONES: 4–8

TYPE: Perennial

LIGHT: Full sun or part shade

SIZE: 4 feet tall, 2 feet wide

INTEREST: Nectar-rich purple flower spikes that attract bees, butterflies, and hummingbirds

USES: Culinary, cut flowers, decorative, medicinal

how to use

The purple flower spikes of anise hyssop make lovely cut flowers and look handsome in a vase with other summer blooms. The dried flowers and leaves can be added to potpourri or used to make a refreshing anise-flavored tea. The fresh leaves and flowers are a spicy addition to salads and make a tea with a slightly sharper flavor than do dried leaves alone. The flowers add color and flavor to fruit pies, or try them with other edible flowers for a pretty garnish.

HOLLYHOCK

how to grow

Hollyhocks thrive in ordinary, well-drained soil and prefer the warmer spots in the garden. In ideal conditions, new shoots arise from the crown of the original plant, allowing an individual clump to produce flowers for a few more years. Self-sown plants are freely produced, ensuring hollyhock's presence in the garden. Space new plants far enough apart to ensure good air circulation. Most varieties require staking. Remove and destroy leaves diseased with hollyhock rust (yellow areas on upper leaf, orange dots underneath). Trim plants to the ground after blooming and remove all leaves and stems from the garden every fall. Pick off Japanese beetles, snails, slugs, and caterpillars by hand.

These tall, stately plants have long had a traditional place at the back of the border or herb garden. During their first year, the plants produce a low clump of rough foliage. The following year, each plant develops three to six strong stalks that reach up to 8 feet tall. Each stem is studded with buds that open from the bottom up to create huge, richly colored spikes of large, showy flowers with papery, overlapping petals. Hollyhock blossoms can be single or double and come in a wide range of colors, including red, pink, yellow, tan, and maroon.

how to use

Collect flowers as they open, and snip off and discard the bitter-tasting base of the petals. Dip in light batter and fry, or brew the petals in hot water for a tea traditionally used as a remedy for indigestion or sore throat. The purple petals of *Alcea* 'Nigra' add smoothness and a dark tea-like color to herbal teas.

ALCEA ROSEA

ZONES: 4–9

TYPE: Biennial or short-lived perennial

LIGHT: Full sun

SIZE: 4–8 feet tall, up to 2 feet wide

INTEREST: Tall spikes of large flowers in every color

USES: Culinary, decorative

CHIVES

how to grow

Chives prefer full sun and a soil that is rich, moist, and well drained, but they are more tolerant of wet, heavy soil and shade than most alliums. The plants are easy to grow and multiply quickly. To renew older clumps, divide every 3 to 4 years, keeping a cluster of at least six bulbs per division. Snipping individual leaves encourages new growth all season long. To grow a new crop of foliage, cut the leaves back to the ground after flowering.

Propagate from seeds or by division in spring or fall. Chives are free of pests and diseases. Some gardeners report that carrots and parsley taste better when grown near a clump of chives.

This tough, clump-forming perennial looks pretty near the front of a flower border, where you can snip leaves and flowers as needed for salads and cooking. The 10-inch-long, onion-scented dark green leaves are hollow and add zest to many dishes. Chives belong to the same family as onions, but they produce many little bulbils from which emerge the characteristic foliage and erect flower stems. The 1-inch, globe-shaped lavender flowers are as tasty as they are decorative.

ALLIUM SCHOENOPRASUM

ZONES: 3–9

TYPE: Perennial

LIGHT: Full sun or part shade

SIZE: 1 foot tall, 1 foot wide

INTEREST: Pink to light purple pompon-like flowers crowning a clump of narrow, hollow leaves

USES: Culinary, decorative, medicinal

how to use

The flowers, bulbs, and foliage of chives lend a light onion flavor to salads and many other dishes. Add the chopped leaves to cream cheese or sour cream to make a tasty spread or dip. Use leaves and flowers as a decorative garnish for soups, stews, salads, omelettes, and baked potatoes. Freeze chopped leaves for winter use.

LEMON VERBENA

how to grow

Plant in well-drained soil, and water regularly, saturating the base and letting the soil dry before watering again. Lemon verbena can rot if its roots stay wet for too long.

Harvest regularly to encourage bushiness, as it is prone to legginess. Prune the dead branches in late spring. Propagate by cuttings rather than by seed.

Originally from South America, lemon verbena thrives in heat with lots of sun. It can withstand brief periods of cold, though it will drop its leaves and go dormant. In colder climates, lemon verbena can be grown in pots brought inside for the winter.

how to use

Use fresh leaves to make tea and flavored oils, syrups, and liqueurs. Dry leaves until they're crumbly, and use them sprinkled on meats and vegetables.

ALOYSIA TRIPHYLLUM

ZONES: 8–11

TYPE: Perennial in warmer zones; annual in cooler ones

LIGHT: Full sun in colder climates

SIZE: 5–6 feet

INTEREST: Fragrant foliage

USES: Culinary, decorative

DILL

how to grow

Dill does best in full sun and loose, fertile well-drained soil amended with compost. Since it does not like to be transplanted, seeds should be sown where you want the plants to grow. Sow in early spring in the North, in late fall and winter in the South. Dill often self-sows. Sow once in spring if you are growing dill for its seeds, since dill planted early in the season will send up a flower stalk, or bolt, in the heat of summer. Sow at monthly intervals until midsummer to ensure a continuous harvest of leaves. Black swallowtail butterfly caterpillars feast on dill, so plant enough for you and for them. For impact and fullness, dill looks best grown in clusters of several plants each.

Dill looks good and tastes even better. Often associated with pickles, the flavor of dill seeds is sharp and spicy. The delicate foliage is as tasty as the seeds and is used to season dips, breads, and other dishes. From spring to early summer, the neat gray-green mound of fragrant foliage adds a delicate texture to the garden. In midsummer, the plant sends up a strong stem topped with large yellow flower heads. With its ferny leaves, strong scent, and large open umbels of yellow flowers, dill adds charm to both ornamental and edible gardens.

ANETHUM GRAVEOLENS

ZONES: All

TYPE: Annual

LIGHT: Full sun

SIZE: 3–5 feet tall, 1 foot wide

INTEREST: Fine, feathery foliage crowned with airy umbels of tiny yellow flowers that attract bees

USES: Culinary, decorative, medicinal

how to use

The cut flowers of dill add interest to summer arrangements or can be added as seasoning to vegetable recipes or baked goods. Its seeds and leaves are popular ingredients in pickles and in Indian and Scandinavian cuisines. For a scrumptious vegetable dip, mix minced dill leaves with sour cream or yogurt, or add fresh dill weed to purchased ranch or onion dip.

ANGELICA

how to grow

Angelica requires rich, moist soil in part sun to light shade. If the plants fail to bloom, the clumps can be divided to encourage flowering. Plant the divisions 3 feet apart. Angelica frequently self-sows; volunteer seedlings should be transplanted in early spring before the long taproot develops. To prolong the life of these short-lived perennials, cut off the blossoms before they produce seeds. Angelica should be mulched to keep the roots moist and cool. It does not do well in areas with hot summers.

Bold clumps of coarse-textured compound leaves and spheres of starry flowers make angelica a distinctive addition to any garden. It is a dramatic, sculptural plant growing up to 6 feet tall. In its first season, the plant puts out a rosette of dark green leaves. In its second year, angelica produces strong ribbed stalks topped with spheres of tiny greenish yellow flowers held high above the leaves.

how to use

Angelica has a mild, sweet licorice flavor. Harvest leaves from spring to summer, stems in early summer. Use the fresh leaves in salads, or cook the leaves and stems as a vegetable. The candied flower stems (see page 124) are delightful when sliced and added to desserts. This herb is also used as a natural sweetener in rhubarb dishes. The aromatic seeds are useful in perfumery, while the roots and seeds add flavor to some liqueurs.

CAUTION: Angelica may cause skin rashes. The plant should be consumed sparingly and is not recommended during pregnancy or for those with diabetes.

ANGELICA ARCHANGELICA

ZONES: 4–7

TYPE: Biennial or short-lived perennial

LIGHT: Part sun to light shade

SIZE: 3–6 feet tall, 3 feet wide

INTEREST: Tall, strong stalks with umbels of greenish white flowers

USES: Culinary, decorative, medicinal

CHERVIL

how to grow

Plant chervil as a cool-season crop in late spring (2 weeks before the last frost) or fall from seed in rich soil with lots of compost. Transplanting will cause it to bolt, so sew seeds where the plant will be growing. Seeds don't keep well, so use fresh seeds each year. Water regularly.

A member of the parsley family (and alternatively known as French parsley), chervil is one of the herbs used in the French mix *fines herbes*, along with tarragon, chives, and parsley.

ANTHRISCUS CEREFOLIUM

ZONES: All

TYPE: Cool-season annual or biennial

LIGHT: Sun to partial shade

SIZE: 12–24 inches tall, 6–12 inches wide

INTEREST: Petite white flowers and glossy foliage

USES: Culinary, medicinal

how to use

Chervil has a slightly licorice flavor and is more subtly flavored than parsley. It doesn't hold up well to lengthy cooking, so add it to meats, soups, and sauces just before serving. Medicinally, it has been used to aid in digestion and lower high blood pressure and as a mild stimulant. Aching joints may be relieved by applying fresh leaves in a warm poultice.

FRENCH TARRAGON

how to grow

French tarragon is a vigorous plant that needs little care other than shearing the stems to the ground in spring before new growth begins. The plants thrive in full sun and well-drained soil, and need extra water only during very dry periods. Mulch roots in winter to protect them from heaving of the soil, and divide every few years to retain vigor. French tarragon does not set seeds; propagate by division or root cutting.

Grown for its aromatic, pungent flavor, French tarragon is a favorite culinary herb. This spreading perennial has dark green, aromatic leaves. The species name, *dracunculus,* derives from tarragon's ancient reputation as a dragon herb; it was said that it would heal toxic bites and stings. The flavorless leaves of Russian tarragon, *Artemisia dracunculus,* have no culinary value.

how to use

An indispensable ingredient of *sauce béarnaise* and *fines herbes*, French tarragon also adds a classy touch to egg, chicken, and fish dishes as well as herbal mustards and vinegars. Harvest sprigs as needed from spring to fall to use fresh, dried, or frozen.

CAUTION: In medicines and aromatherapy, tarragon is said to aid digestion and menstrual problems. For this reason it is not recommended for use during pregnancy.

ARTEMISIA DRACUNCULUS VAR. SATIVA

ZONES: 3–8

TYPE: Perennial

LIGHT: Full sun

SIZE: 2 feet tall, 2 feet wide

INTEREST: Abundant, smooth, fragrant foliage on upright, branched stems

USES: Aromatic, culinary

ENGLISH DAISY

how to grow

Native to Europe, English daisies grow well in a wide range of conditions but prefer moist, well-drained, fertile soil in full sun to part shade. To lengthen the period of bloom, remove the spent flowers and provide some shade in midafternoon where summers are hot. Propagate by sowing seeds directly in the garden in fall for bloom the following spring, or start seeds indoors in late winter and set plants in the garden after the last frost.

This charming little plant looks perfect along the edge of a border or path or planted among spring bulbs in a rock garden or container. Traditionally, English daisies have also been planted in lawns, where the green grass serves as a background for the tidy flowers that bloom from spring to fall. The plentiful 1-inch blossoms have a central yellow disk surrounded by abundant petal-shaped ray flowers. Leaves are small and obovate, arranged in a basal rosette from which the daisies rise on short, supple stems.

BELLIS PERENNIS

ZONES: 8–10

TYPE: Perennial often grown as an annual or biennial

LIGHT: Full sun or part shade

SIZE: 6 inches tall, 6 inches wide

INTEREST: Small, daisy-like flowers sitting above a rosette of dark green leaves

USES: Culinary, decorative, medicinal

how to use

Use the buds, ray flowers, and leaves of English daisy to add a sharp, fresh taste to salads, or cook the leaves for a green vegetable. The plant was a popular topical balm for joint pain and bruising in England during the sixteenth century.

BORAGO OFFICINALIS

ZONES: All

TYPE: Annual

LIGHT: Full sun

SIZE: 2–3 feet tall, 1–2 feet wide

INTEREST: Open clusters of blue flowers attractive to honeybees

USES: Culinary, decorative, medicinal

BORAGE

how to grow

A native of the Mediterranean region, borage does best in full sun and well-drained soil that has been amended with some compost or rotted manure. Propagate by sowing seeds in pots and transplanting to the garden in spring, or direct-sow in early spring. Space plants 15 inches apart. Borage often self-sows if allowed to go to seed. The plants look and taste best before and during blossoming. Borage deteriorates after blooming and becomes mildew prone in warm, humid conditions. In hot climates with long summers, repeat sowings for a continual supply of fresh, handsome plants. Once flowers have gone by, the plants should be removed from the garden. Japanese beetles may appear on the leaves in summer. Remove them by hand in the morning, when they are sluggish, and drop in a can of soapy water.

Borage has a bushy habit with dark green leaves and star-shaped lapis blue flowers accented with black stamens. The foliage, stems, and buds are covered with silvery hairs that give the entire plant a soft metallic sheen, making the flowers even more vibrant. It is best placed toward the center of an herb border behind tidier plants. In addition to the pretty flowers, borage leaves, blossoms, and stems add a light, refreshing taste to baked dishes and summer salads.

how to use

Fresh borage leaves add a delightful, subtle taste to cool summer drinks. If you don't mind the bristly texture of the fresh plant, use chopped borage leaves to add a cucumber-like flavor to garden salads. The flavorful young leaves can be cooked as a vegetable, or chopped finely and blended with cream cheese for a tasty spread. Candy the flowers or add to a variety of vegetable dishes as a garnish. Toss a handful of the blossoms over fruit salad or use to decorate frosted cakes. They also can be frozen in ice cubes for a bright addition to drinks. Borage leaves are best when used fresh, since they do not dry or freeze well.

POT MARIGOLD

how to grow

Pot marigold is a versatile plant that does well in full sun and a wide range of soils. Sow the large seeds directly in the garden in early spring. When the seedlings are about 4 inches high, thin to 12 inches apart. Deadhead to increase the number of blooms and prolong flowering. The plants freely self-sow if allowed to go to seed. Pot marigold does best in cool weather.

In the North, the blooms appear in summer, but in the South, this plant flowers best in the cooler seasons of spring and fall. Powdery mildew sometimes covers the leaves with a whitish coating in late summer. If this disease is a problem in your area, plant pot marigold in a breezy part of the garden, spacing the plants 14 inches apart.

The cheerful blooms of pot marigold make a bright addition to any garden. Measuring up to 3 inches across, the blossoms are either single or double and range in color from cream to yellow and gold to orange. These vigorous, bushy plants grow wider throughout the season, filling spaces left open by other flowers since gone by with sunny, summer colors.

CALENDULA OFFICINALIS

ZONES: All

TYPE: Annual

LIGHT: Full sun

SIZE: Up to 2 feet tall, 1 foot wide

INTEREST: Brightly colored, daisy-like flowers on long-branched stems

USES: Culinary, decorative

how to use

Pot marigolds are excellent cut flowers, adding bright shades to summer and fall arrangements. They also dry well for everlasting bouquets. The petals can be brewed into a fine tea, eaten fresh in salads, or dried into a powder and used to impart a saffron color to foods. The petals can also be blended into skin creams to soothe skin rashes.

ROMAN CHAMOMILE

how to grow

Chamomile thrives in full sun and fertile, sandy soil amended with some organic matter. Soils high in nitrogen produce plants with fewer flowers and less fragrant foliage. Chamomile prefers cool summers and even moisture; it can tolerate short periods of drought. To propagate, sow seeds in spring or divide in fall. Space plants 6 to 12 inches apart. Remove spent flowers to encourage continued bloom and to inhibit self-sowing unless you are growing a chamomile lawn.

Chamomile is a low, spreading plant with aromatic, feathery foliage and abundant daisy-like flowers from summer to fall. The matlike plants make a lovely ground cover for sunny places and add a delicate touch to herb and flower borders. Because of its fragrance, chamomile works well planted in pots placed where you can easily smell the aromatic blossoms and foliage. Sitting on chamomile-covered seats or walking on chamomile lawns or chamomile-lined paths also releases the plant's pleasant, enchanting scent.

how to use

Dried chamomile flowers make a soothing tea that is said to relieve indigestion, induce restful sleep, and relieve fever, insomnia, menstrual pain, and digestive problems. Dry the blossoms on a paper towel or screen. Make certain that blossoms are dry before storing them in tightly closed jars. Chamomile tea, applied as a rinse, can lighten blond hair and may prolong the life of cut flowers when added to the water. Spraying cool chamomile tea on the leaves of phlox and other garden plants is said to control powdery mildew.

CHAMAEMELUM NOBILE

ZONES: 4–8

TYPE: Perennial

LIGHT: Full sun

SIZE: 6 inches tall, 12 inches wide

INTEREST: Delicate, daisy-like blossoms and fine, apple-scented leaves

USES: Decorative, medicinal

FEVERFEW

how to grow

Feverfew is easy to grow in full sun. It requires well-drained soil and regular watering. The plants are quite vigorous and self-sow freely, though any volunteers can be easily weeded out. To control their spread, cut the plants back after flowering. Propagate species from seeds or cuttings, or by division, setting plants 3 to 4 feet apart. If aphids become a problem, wash them from the plant with a stream of water from a hose.

Feverfew is a bushy, short-lived perennial with finely cut light green foliage and sprays of small daisies in summer, especially where the season is cool. The leaves have a strong, pungent aroma. A native of southeastern Europe to the Caucasus, this old-fashioned plant also comes in double-flowered and gold-leaved varieties.

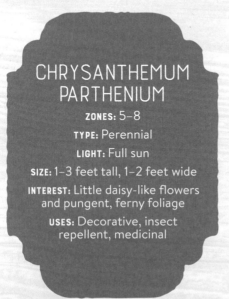

CHRYSANTHEMUM PARTHENIUM

ZONES: 5–8

TYPE: Perennial

LIGHT: Full sun

SIZE: 1–3 feet tall, 1–2 feet wide

INTEREST: Little daisy-like flowers and pungent, ferny foliage

USES: Decorative, insect repellent, medicinal

how to use

Feverfew makes an excellent long-lasting cut flower. Dried blooms are suitable for teas, potpourris, and flower arrangements. An important herb in colonial gardens, feverfew derives its name from its traditional use, lowering fevers. Other traditional medicinal uses include relief of headaches, arthritis, and rheumatism. When added to soups and stews, feverfew imparts an astringent, bitter flavor. The aromatic leaves are sometimes used as an insect repellent, although the plant can cause a skin rash in some people.

CAUTION: The excessive internal use of feverfew is discouraged by herbalists; the plant should not be used during pregnancy.

CILANTRO/CORIANDER

how to grow

Cilantro grows well in light, well-drained soil in full sun. Because it doesn't like to be moved, sow seeds in spring where you want the plants to grow. Thin seedlings to 4 to 6 inches apart. Foliage is best when the weather is cool. Provide some afternoon shade in hot climates to protect the leaves from drying out. Plants bolt quickly when the weather turns hot and dry, an advantage if you're growing the plant for its seeds. To maintain your cilantro supply, reseed every 2 to 4 weeks beginning in spring and continuing through summer. Planting coriander near fennel may keep the fennel from setting many seeds.

Cilantro is a staple of Mexican and Indian cuisines. It is also used in Chinese cooking, hence its other common name, Chinese parsley. The leaves of the plant are known as cilantro, the seeds as coriander. The small white to lavender flowers are attractive, yet the plant grows so fast and goes to seed so quickly that cilantro's ornamental effect is short-lived. The leaves at the base of the plant are lobed and soft-textured, while those on the flower stem are feathery. Grow cilantro with other kitchen herbs, where you can do repeated sowings for a continuous harvest of this pungent, strong-scented herb.

how to use

The flowers, leaves, and roots are all used to flavor soups, salsas, and other spicy dishes. Coriander seeds are tasty in sweets and liqueurs and ground into curry powder. Allow them to turn pale brown on the plant, then harvest. The flavor of dried cilantro leaves cannot compare with the dusky heat of the fresh herb, so freeze fresh leaves for later culinary use (see page 243).

CORIANDRUM SATIVUM

ZONES: All
TYPE: Annual
LIGHT: Full sun
SIZE: 1–3 feet tall, 1 foot wide
INTEREST: Aromatic leaves and clusters of white or lavender flowers
USES: Aromatic, culinary

LEMONGRASS

how to grow

Plant starts of lemongrass outside after the last frost of spring in well-drained soil where they will get full sun. Maintain consistent moisture so that the roots don't dry out. To harvest, cut the stalks right at the ground, in order to get the bulbous part. Lemongrass is fairly pest- and disease-free.

Known mostly for its use in Asian cooking, lemongrass is a fast-growing ornamental grass with graceful arched leaves that enhance borders, walkways, and containers whether harvested for cooking or medicinal uses or not.

CYMBOPOGON CITRATUS

ZONES: 9–11

TYPE: Perennial grown as an annual

LIGHT: Full sun

SIZE: 3–6 feet tall, 4 feet wide

INTEREST: Lemon fragrance of leaves when brushed

USES: Culinary, medicinal, decorative

how to use

Resembling a large scallion, lemongrass is used in Southeast Asian cooking. Use the whole thing to flavor soups and stews (then remove before serving), or cut it up to add its sweet, lemony flavor to dishes. Lemongrass has been used medicinally to treat a wide range of symptoms, from high blood pressure, insomnia, and anxiety to headaches, fevers, and diarrhea.

CLOVE PINK

how to grow

Clove pink thrives in rich, well-drained soil with a neutral to slightly alkaline pH. It benefits from being cut back after blooming. The roots prefer to be evenly moist, while the foliage and flowers do best in warm, dry conditions. In humid locations, clove pink can suffer viral and fungal diseases that weaken the plants, opening the way for infestations of aphids, thrips, and spider mites. To propagate, start seeds indoors in late winter or divide established plants in late summer.

Clove pink has dainty, fringed deep pink blossoms that glow against mounds of silvery blue-green stems and narrow foliage. What stands out most about this plant, in addition to its charming appearance, is its spicy fragrance. Although this species includes the large-bloomed florists' carnations, these have no fragrance.

how to use

Cut flowers in midmorning for bouquets, or dry them for use in potpourri. The raw petals, minus the bitter white base, add a delightful floral flavor to salads. Use the petals as an ingredient in herbal butter, or candy them (see page 124) to decorate desserts. The petals add a spicy flavor to wines and vinegar, and make a sweet syrup when boiled with sugar and water.

DIANTHUS CARYOPHYLLUS

ZONES: 8–10

TYPE: Perennial often grown as an annual

LIGHT: Full sun

SIZE: 1–2 feet tall, less than 1 foot wide

INTEREST: Pretty pink to purple flowers against glaucous blue-green leaves

USES: Aromatic, culinary, decorative

PURPLE CONEFLOWER

how to grow

Purple coneflower is a rugged plant that thrives in a range of soils and is heat and drought tolerant. Do not fertilize, because the plants may become floppy and require staking. Propagate by dividing clumps in spring or fall. Space plants 18 to 24 inches apart to promote good air circulation, which inhibits the growth of mildew on the leaves. Old, thick clumps can be thinned by division or selective pruning. If Japanese beetles are a problem, pick them off by hand and drop them in a jar of soapy water.

The spiky, pointed orange disk of the purple coneflower gives this stately herb its other name, hedgehog coneflower. Its rough dark green foliage contrasts handsomely with its 3- to 4-inch daisy-like blooms that range in color from icy white to burgundy, depending on the cultivar. Purple coneflower's strong, erect habit, coarse foliage, and majestic blossoms lend a bold presence when massed in the border or planted in rows in a cutting garden. This native herb provides a nectar source in butterfly gardens and wildflower meadows.

ECHINACEA PURPUREA

ZONES: 4–8

TYPE: Perennial

LIGHT: Full sun

SIZE: 3–4 feet tall, 2 feet wide

INTEREST: Drooping, rosy purple ray flowers around a dark bronze central cone

USES: Decorative, medicinal

how to use

Purple coneflower makes an excellent long-lasting cut flower. Its seed heads look equally striking in fresh and dry arrangements. This native herb, which still grows wild in the prairies and fields of the central United States, was used for centuries as a medicine by native North Americans, particularly the Plains Indians. The dried roots are used to stimulate the immune system and can help reduce the severity of cold and flu symptoms. The roots are lifted and dried in fall to make medicinal powders, tinctures, and infusions.

CAUTION: People with immune-system disorders such as diabetes or AIDS must check with their doctors before using purple coneflower.

FENNEL

how to grow

Fennel prefers full sun and well-drained alkaline soil amended with organic matter. Propagate from seeds sown in early spring or fall. In warmer areas where fennel is a perennial, divide in spring. Deadhead flowers to keep plants from self-sowing. Grow fennel as far away from coriander as possible, since this herb is reported to inhibit seed formation in fennel. Although fennel will not harm dill, keep these plants apart because of their tendency to cross-fertilize.

Fennel stands tall in the garden, with its threadlike shiny leaves and hollow stems towering over many other kitchen herbs. The broad umbels of flat yellow summer flowers give way to sweet anise-flavored brown seeds in fall. Attractive though fennel is, consider carefully where you grow it, since its presence may have a detrimental effect on the size and viability of other garden plants, including many vegetables and herbs.

how to use

Fennel is an herb with many uses. The anise-scented yellow flowers are long-lasting additions to fresh flower arrangements. The seeds and leaves make an excellent herb tea and add a flavorful accent to soups, stews, and stuffings. In addition, the seeds can be chewed as a breath sweetener and to curb hunger pangs. Fennel has been used to relieve flatulence, increase the supply of mother's milk, encourage weight loss, and as an aphrodisiac.

FOENICULUM VULGARE

ZONES: 6–9

TYPE: Biennial or perennial grown as an annual

LIGHT: Full sun

SIZE: Up to 6 feet tall, 2 feet wide

INTEREST: Large, flat yellow flower heads and fragrant, needle-thin foliage

USES: Aromatic, culinary, decorative

SWEET WOODRUFF

how to grow

Sweet woodruff prefers a shady location in the South, where it is evergreen in winter and may die back in summer. In the North, it requires at least part shade; the deep green summer foliage dies and dries to a warm tan in winter. A woodland species, sweet woodruff thrives in moist, rich acidic soil beneath the canopies of deciduous trees. It even grows well near pines and hemlocks, where most other plants falter. The plant spreads easily, especially when adequate moisture is provided. Virtually carefree, sweet woodruff makes an excellent ground cover. The seeds are difficult to germinate; instead, set out starter plants in spring or fall. Propagate by division in spring or fall.

In late spring, sweet woodruff bears loose clusters of tiny four-petaled vanilla-scented flowers on slender stems. In winter, the abundant green leaves turn tan, adding subtle interest to the landscape. The species name, *odoratum*, means "fragrant." The flowers and foliage have the scent of vanilla when cut or dried.

GALIUM ODORATUM

ZONES: 4–8

TYPE: Perennial

LIGHT: Full to part shade

SIZE: 1-foot-tall ground cover

INTEREST: Fragrant, starry white flowers on a spreading mat of whorled rich green leaves

USES: Aromatic, decorative

how to use

Unlike many other herbs, which are most aromatic when fresh, the leaves of sweet woodruff become increasingly fragrant as they dry. An ingredient in Alsatian May wine, sweet woodruff can also be mixed with other fragrant plants in potpourri (although its crumbly nature may make the potpourri look a little dusty). The aromatic dried leaves were strewn onto floors to sweeten the air in medieval dwellings.

SUNFLOWER

how to grow

Sunflowers like well-drained soil in full sun. Sow seeds in the garden about one-half inch deep in spring after the last frost. Thin seedlings to stand 12 inches apart. Keep well watered and mulch around the base of the plants to keep the soil cool.

Sunflowers are perky, vigorous plants that add architectural interest to the garden and attract birds and butterflies. Revered by the ancient Incas in Peru and cultivated by Native Americans for more than three thousand years, this native plant is still beloved by children and adults alike. On sunny days the large flower heads follow the sun across the sky. Sunflower seeds are easy to plant, germinate quickly, and grow fast, making this plant a favorite for children's gardens. The cheerful yellow blossoms give way to seed-filled flower heads that become hubs of activity for hungry birds, squirrels, and people.

how to use

The small-flowered types of sunflower look terrific in bouquets. The seeds of the mammoth varieties can be ground into meal, Native American–style, or eaten raw or toasted, as a snack. The seeds lend a nutty taste to baked products, and their oil is used for cooking and salad dressings. Consuming sunflower seeds is said to help lower blood cholesterol levels.

HELIANTHUS ANNUUS

ZONES: All

TYPE: Annual

LIGHT: Full sun

SIZE: Up to 10 feet tall, 1–2 feet wide

INTEREST: Very large, drooping flower heads with yellow ray flowers and dark centers on tall, thick stalks

USES: Culinary, decorative

CURRY PLANT

how to grow

A native of the Mediterranean region, curry plant grows best in raised beds or in full sun and loose, well-drained, sandy soil. In areas where they are perennial, the plants are susceptible to root rot during moist winters. Although regular watering stimulates growth, the plant can tolerate periods of dry weather. Prune back the side stems to encourage branching. Aphids and mealybugs may be a problem, especially during periods of warm, humid weather. Propagate from cuttings in spring or late summer.

During the summer months, curry plant looks like a small silver bush with its needlelike pewter gray foliage and 2-inch terminal clusters of dark yellow flower heads. During the colder months, the everlasting blossoms add summer beauty to dried arrangements. The plant looks wonderful in a pot on the patio, where you can appreciate its appearance and fragrance close up. Curry plant derives its common name from its aromatic leaves, which smell like Indian curry powder. It is not, however, the source of curry powder, which is a blend of several spices.

HELICHRYSUM ANGUSTIFOLIUM

ZONES: 9–10

TYPE: Perennial grown as an annual

LIGHT: Full sun

SIZE: 2 feet tall, 2 feet wide

INTEREST: Dark yellow everlasting flowers on a silvery, fragrant bushy plant

USES: Aromatic, decorative, medicinal

how to use

Cut and dry everlasting flowers for use in dried arrangements. Harvest tender young leaves from spring to fall to use fresh in salads, or add to cooked dishes for a light curry taste.

HEMEROCALLIS

ZONES: 4–9

TYPE: Perennial

LIGHT: Full sun to part shade

SIZE: 10–60 inches tall, up to 30 inches wide; blossoms 2–9 inches across

INTEREST: Colorful blooms rise above a mound of elegant, straplike foliage

USES: Culinary, decorative

DAYLILY

how to grow

Daylilies thrive in full sun but also do very well in part shade. They like loose, well-drained fertile soil. Water regularly for maximum growth. Spacing holes 1 to 2 feet apart, dig a hole 2 feet wide and 1 foot deep for each plant. Mix a shovelful of compost, humus, or aged manure into the removed soil and use to backfill. Mulch around the plants to maintain moisture content and encourage growth.

Evergreen varieties generally perform better in the South, while dormant kinds do best in the North. Divide daylilies when plants become crowded or when the flowers grow sparse. Daylilies are mostly pest- and disease-free and are easily propagated by division in spring or fall. However, one of the best things about daylilies is that they can grow forever without requiring division.

Daylilies are among the most elegant of plants, easy to grow, and wonderfully tasty. Blossom shapes range from the classic trumpet to a delicate spidery form. The season of bloom varies with the species or cultivar, from March in the South to August and September in the North. Some hybrids, such as 'Stella de Oro', 'Black-Eyed Stella', and lemony 'Happy Returns', bloom all summer long. Daylily habits also vary from circular mounds to spreading ground covers. The plants look great in tubs, in massed plantings, and in mixed borders. Colors vary, but the tastiest varieties are yellow.

how to use

Daylily buds, flowers, inner leaves, and crisp root tubers can be boiled, sautéed, or stir-fried, or chopped raw for salads. Flowers, without pistil and stamens, make edible garnishes. The buds contain significant amounts of protein and vitamins A and C and are a popular ingredient in Oriental cuisine. The flowers are edible until the day after bloom; used any later, they taste bitter. The stronger the fragrance, the more flavorful the flower.

HYSSOP

how to grow

This pest-free Mediterranean native grows well in dry, sandy, slightly acidic to alkaline soil in full sun. Spring is the best time to clip hyssop into hedges. Propagate from softwood cuttings in summer, or from seeds or by root division in spring and fall. Hyssop is a slow-growing plant, so start seeds indoors for spring cultivation. Cut the plants to the ground in spring, or in mild climates, after blooming.

Hyssop has two distinct and lovely garden personalities. It makes a low, boxy, semi-ever-green hedge suitable for knot gardens or formal edging, with plants spaced 12 to 15 inches apart and sheared. Spaced 2 feet apart and allowed to grow freely, hyssop has a relaxed, shrubby habit and bears spikes of blue or, rarely, white or pink flowers that grow in whorls from the leaf axils. Hyssop is woody at the base, and its stems are covered with shiny, narrow dark green leaves that release a powerful musky-mint aroma when touched. In biblical times it was considered one of the purifying herbs.

HYSSOPUS OFFICINALIS

ZONES: 3–9

TYPE: Perennial

LIGHT: Full sun

SIZE: 2 feet tall, 2 feet wide

INTEREST: Blue, pink, or white flower spikes that attract bees and butterflies

USES: Aromatic, culinary, decorative, medicinal

how to use

Hyssop flowers are useful for fresh arrangements. Harvest the tops of the stems, including flowers, when they begin to bloom. When growing hyssop for tea, cut stems to the ground before flowering and dry the leaves whole. After flowering, this plant becomes increasingly woody and loses some of its aroma. Used sparingly, hyssop flowers, stems, and leaves add zest to soups, meats, vegetables, salads, and fruit pies. Hyssop is also an ingredient in perfumes and liqueurs, especially Chartreuse.

CAUTION: Traditionally, hyssop aids digestion and repels insects, but it is not recommended for use during pregnancy.

SWEET BAY

how to grow

Native to the Mediterranean region, sweet bay prefers well-drained, average soil and consistent moisture. Once established, it can tolerate some dryness but requires protection from cold winds and icy weather. In northern areas, grow bay in a container so that you can bring it indoors before the first frost. For container plants, use a potting mix that is about one-half potting soil, one-quarter peat moss, and one-quarter screened garden soil. Fertilize in late winter or spring, as new growth begins, and again in late summer. Sweet bay is not easy to propagate; try using stem cuttings taken in fall. Expect to wait 6 to 9 months for roots to develop.

Aromatic sweet bay leaves grow on evergreen plants that can rise as tall as 30 feet. Allowed to grow freely, their natural habit is upright and boldly attractive, with handsome leaves that are smooth, dark green, and shiny, with a prominent light midvein. Small, light yellow flowers appear in the leaf axils in spring, followed by black berries later in the growing season. Because its roots tolerate confinement, sweet bay also makes an excellent potted plant or topiary. In ancient Greece, sweet bay, also known as laurel, crowned the brows of poets and heroes, making it a truly noble herb.

how to use

Leafy twigs of laurel add texture and fragrance to herbal wreaths and dried arrangements. The essential oil in bay leaves enhances the flavor of soups, stews, and sauces, both alone and as an ingredient in a *bouquet garni*. The aroma of bay grows more potent when dried and crushed or powdered. Bay leaves are spicier dried than fresh and remain flavorful for about a year.

A tea made from dried or fresh bay leaves has traditionally been used to increase the appetite and aid digestion.

LAURUS NOBILIS

ZONES: 8–10

TYPE: Perennial shrub

LIGHT: Full sun to part shade

SIZE: Up to 30 feet tall, 25 feet wide

INTEREST: Stiff, glossy dark green leaves on a handsome shrub or medium-sized tree

USES: Aromatic, culinary, decorative

ENGLISH LAVENDER

how to grow

This pest-free plant thrives in full sun and likes well-drained, slightly acidic to slightly alkaline sandy soil. In mild climates, lavender becomes a woody, bushy evergreen that can be pruned at any time of year. In cold climates, however, the plant needs to be pruned to about 6 inches high or cut back near the ground if it becomes woody and unkempt. To keep lavender disease-free, provide full sun and good air circulation. To avoid root rot in heavy soil, plant lavender in raised beds so that water will not collect. Propagate by layering, by division, or from cuttings in summer.

The distinctive aroma of lavender—familiar from soaps and perfumes—recalls the clean, sweet freshness of a warm summer morning. Planted as a low hedge or as a bushy edging along paths or walkways, lavender releases its pleasant fragrance when brushed. Massed in a perennial or mixed border, it blends with other plants and softens the strong aspect of bold colors. This Mediterranean native is drought-tolerant and grows well on dry, sunny slopes.

LAVANDULA ANGUSTIFOLIA

ZONES: 5–9

TYPE: Perennial

LIGHT: Full sun

SIZE: 2–3 feet tall, 3 feet wide

INTEREST: Clumps of perfumed silvery green foliage and bright blue-purple flowering spikes

USES: Aromatic, culinary, decorative

how to use

Harvest lavender flowers as they begin to open, when their fragrance is most intense. Lavender is a wonderful long-lasting cut flower. Dried, it adds fragrance to potpourris and sachets. A small lavender-filled muslin pillow may relieve sleeplessness and soothe the jitters. The oil of *L. angustifolia*, the most fragrant lavender, is a common ingredient in soaps and perfumes. The fresh flowers also add a unique flavor to desserts, baked goods, vinegars, and jellies.

LEVISTICUM OFFICINALE

ZONES: 3–8

TYPE: Perennial

LIGHT: Full sun to part shade

SIZE: Up to 6 feet tall, about 4 feet wide

INTEREST: Yellow-green flower clusters rising above a leafy, hollow-stemmed plant that smells like celery

USES: Aromatic, culinary, medicinal, decorative

LOVAGE

how to grow

Lovage prefers a sunny to partly shady location in rich, moist soil amended with some organic matter. If you're growing lovage for its leaves and want a fuller look, remove the flower heads before they bloom. After flowering, the celery-scented leaves may turn yellow and become tasteless, so give your plant sufficient nutrients through compost and organic fertilizers to ensure good health. Lovage needs little attention once established, but it is susceptible to leaf miners, which can be handled by removing the affected foliage. Divide in spring or plant seeds outdoors in autumn.

Lovage is a bold plant that looks striking at the back of the border. In summer, shiny yellow-green triple-compound leaves drape a scaffold of strong stems that support decorative clusters of tiny yellow flowers. The entire plant, including flowers, seeds, stems, leaves, and roots, is edible; it tastes like celery but is much easier to grow. Lovage is sometimes called loveache, in reference to its use as an aphrodisiac during the Middle Ages. Its reputation as a love potion comes not, however, from its powers but rather from the mispronunciation of *liguria*, its common name in Roman times.

how to use

Harvest lovage leaves as needed in summer to add a celery-like, although much stronger, flavor to recipes. Used sparingly to avoid overwhelming the flavor of the food, lovage leaves enhance stuffings, soups, stews, mixed vegetables, and sauces. Add the seeds to baked goods and salad dressings. Harvest the stems in spring to use fresh in salads or cooked as a vegetable. Or chop and candy the stems to add to desserts (see page 124).

Traditionally, lovage was used more for medicine than food. The roots were thought to ease menstrual pain, flatulence, and kidney and digestive problems. Because of its diuretic properties, some herbalists used it to treat obesity.

GERMAN CHAMOMILE

how to grow

This easy-to-grow herb flourishes in ordinary to sandy well-drained soil in full sun. Plants will keep blooming if you harvest blossoms as they open; otherwise, expect them to decline soon after flowering. To propagate German chamomile, sow seeds 6 inches apart in early spring or fall. To take advantage of German chamomile's tendency to self-sow, refrain from harvesting one or more plants and allow them to go to seed.

Although charming and delicate in appearance, German chamomile is hardy and easy to grow—so easy, in fact, that this European and Asian native has naturalized itself in the fields and roadsides of North America. Unlike its low-growing perennial counterpart, Roman chamomile, *Chamaemelum nobile,* German chamomile is unsuitable for a lawn substitute but well adapted for the ornamental herb garden. Its applelike fragrance, feathery foliage, and 1-inch white and yellow flowers contrast nicely with coarser plants such as mint, sage, and parsley. While one plant may go unnoticed in the garden, however, several massed together have a definite, if dainty, presence. For cottage-garden appeal, let random, self-sown chamomile seedlings interweave themselves among other flowering plants.

MATRICARIA RECUTITA

ZONES: All

TYPE: Annual

LIGHT: Full sun

SIZE: 2–2½ feet tall

INTEREST: A fragrant, finely textured plant with yellow-centered daisy-like flowers.

USES: Aromatic, decorative, medicinal

how to use

Although German chamomile is less fragrant than Roman chamomile, it contains slightly more volatile oil, so many herbalists prefer it. Dried chamomile adds a light apple aroma to herbal wreaths and potpourris. It has a relaxing effect when placed in a muslin bag and steeped in warm bathwater. Tea made from chamomile flowers may calm the nerves, soothe insomnia, and relieve indigestion and teething pain. Strong chamomile tea enhances blond highlights when used as a hair rinse. To dry chamomile, harvest the blossoms when they open. Spread on screens to dry in a warm, airy room.

LEMON BALM

how to grow

In rich, moist, well-drained soil, lemon balm will grow and spread with abandon. In less ideal conditions, its habit is more restrained. Cutting back the spent flowers prevents self-seeding and makes the plants bushier and more attractive. Maintain adequate air circulation around lemon balm to avoid powdery mildew.

A member of the square-stemmed mint family, lemon balm forms a spreading clump of loosely branched, crinkled green foliage. Small white to pale yellow flowers grow clustered in leaf axils. Lemon balm, however, is grown more for its scent than its looks. Little hairs emitting a lemony fragrance when brushed cover its heart-shaped scalloped leaves. The plant attracts bees galore. In fact, *Melissa* means "honeybee" in Greek.

how to use

Dry the intensely fragrant leaves of lemon balm in late summer for potpourris and tea. Rub the oil-rich fresh leaves on wood as a natural lemon-scented furniture polish. Or add a cup of fresh leaves to your bathwater for an aromatic, soothing experience. The plant is also a natural insect repellent; rub your skin with lemon balm leaves to help keep bugs away.

Traditionally used as a sedative, in Shakespeare's day lemon balm was dried, cut up, and strewn on the floor for a sweet-smelling home. In the kitchen, the minty lemon flavor of fresh lemon balm complements fruit and green salads, stuffings, seafood, and vegetables, not to mention liqueurs and wines.

Harvest the entire plant at once, just after you notice flower buds. Cut it to within 2 inches of the ground. It will grow back to provide one or two more complete harvests during the season.

MELISSA OFFICINALIS

ZONES: 5–9

TYPE: Perennial

LIGHT: Full sun to part shade

SIZE: 2 feet tall, 2 feet wide

INTEREST: Loose, upright clump of textured green leaves with strong lemon scent and a hint of mint

USES: Aromatic, culinary

PENNYROYAL

how to grow

Pennyroyal grows best in rich, moist, well-drained soil amended with generous amounts of organic matter. Plant in full sun or part shade and water regularly. Cut back flower heads to keep pennyroyal flat and green, or allow the plants to blossom and let them self-sow. Propagate from cuttings or by root division.

Pennyroyal makes an excellent noninvasive ground cover for damp, shady areas. Its thick mat of dark green leaves has a potent citronella scent that repels insects. Because of its low, dense habit, pennyroyal works well in rock gardens or between the steppingstones of garden paths. It even makes an excellent lawn substitute that supports occasional mowing. Little whorls of lilac flowers appear above the small leaves.

MENTHA PULEGIUM

ZONES: 6–9

TYPE: Perennial

LIGHT: Full sun to part shade

SIZE: 6–12 inches tall, with an indefinite spread

INTEREST: Dense, aromatic ground cover of dark green leaves and small lilac-colored flowers

USES: Aromatic, culinary, insect repellent

how to use

The species name, *pulegium*, comes from *pulex*, the Latin word for "flea," in reference to pennyroyal's flea-repelling properties, but it does more than repel fleas. Placed in muslin bags and hung in the closet, pennyroyal repels moths and mice. When rubbed on the skin, it can deter gnats, ticks, flies, chiggers, and mosquitoes. The dried leaves add a fragrant touch to potpourris. The annual American pennyroyal, *Hedeoma pulegioides*, has similar properties and was used for centuries by Native Americans.

CAUTION: Unlike most other mints, pennyroyal should not be taken internally.

BEE BALM

how to grow

Native to damp, rich sites of North America, bee balm thrives in moist, fertile soil in full sun or light shade. Clumps of this naturally vigorous plant spread quickly, often doubling in size in a season. To control its spread, plant bee balm in a container sunk into the ground. As the flowers fade, cut plants back to within a few inches of the ground to control self-seeding and powdery mildew. Divide every few years in spring to rejuvenate clumps.

Bee balm produces plentiful amounts of seeds, but growing it from gathered seeds is a bit of a gamble. Since bees frequently cross-pollinate one type with another, the seeds often produce plants with pale flowers and less aromatic foliage than the parents. Grown from seeds, bee balm will usually flower 2 years after planting.

Bee balm, with its bright red whorls of tubular summer flowers, is a magnet to the eye as well as visiting hummingbirds, bees, and butterflies. Also called Oswego tea, the plant has colorful blossoms held above pointed oval leaves that have a spicy citrus fragrance. Bee balm adds as much interest to the table as it does to the garden. Add the flowers and leaves to salads and hors d'oeuvres, or use it in a vase alone or with other cut flowers.

how to use

Bee balm adds a summertime look to fresh bouquets. Use the delicately flavored flowers fresh in salads and as edible garnishes, or dry them for potpourris. Leaves add a pleasing flavor to fruit salads, jellies, and cold drinks. They make a soothing yet invigorating tea that aids digestion.

MONARDA DIDYMA

ZONES: 4–9

TYPE: Perennial

LIGHT: Full sun to part shade

SIZE: 2–4 feet tall, 3–5 feet wide

INTEREST: Moplike whorls of scarlet flowers that attract hummingbirds, bees, and butterflies

USES: Aromatic, culinary, decorative, medicinal

CATNIP

how to grow

Catnip grows well in average soil in full sun to part shade. This easy-to-grow herb is drought-tolerant, pest- and disease-free, and requires little care. Plants grown in rich, fertile soil can be floppy. All plants, regardless of where they are grown, look tired at the end of the growing season. Control catnip's spread by pulling out or digging up unwanted plants. To prevent self-sowing, deadhead after flowering. Propagate from seeds in spring, by division, or by transplanting self-sown seedlings.

Catnip forms a large, relaxed clump of coarse, triangular gray-green foliage. Its pungent, minty aroma is nearly irresistible to cats. The leaves and stems are covered with a thin layer of white down. In summer, small spikes of pale white flowers appear atop the stems. Catnip belongs to the mint family and, like other mints, has square stems. The vigorous plants spread by rhizomatous roots and by self-sowing and can become invasive.

NEPETA CATARIA

ZONES: 3–8

TYPE: Perennial

LIGHT: Full sun to part shade

SIZE: 2–4 feet tall, 3 feet wide

INTEREST: Bushy, spreading habit with aromatic leaves and spikes of white flowers

USES: Aromatic, medicinal

how to use

Catnip leaves can be gathered anytime but are most potent when the plant begins to flower. The dried leaves are a wonderful filler for cat toys. Catnip tea has a calming, sedative effect and may alleviate cold symptoms.

CAUTION: Catnip is not recommended for use during pregnancy.

SWEET BASIL

how to grow

Basil prefers hot weather, full sun, average to fertile soil, and regular watering. Propagate from seeds sown directly in the garden or started 8 weeks before the last frost. Place plants 12 inches apart. Except for Japanese beetles, which can be removed by hand and drowned in soapy water, basil is pest-free. Pinch off growing tips and flower spikes to make the plant bushier and to encourage the production of even more of its tasty leaves.

Fragrance, flavor, and healing properties make sweet basil a favorite plant for herb gardens. Basil has an erect, bushy habit with branching stems of richly aromatic dark green leaves and small spikes of white or pale purple flowers from summer to fall. In addition to being a mainstay of the herb garden, basil's good looks accent a decorative flower border. It also serves you well in the vegetable garden, where its inclusion can enhance the growth of peppers and tomatoes while repelling asparagus beetles and other pests.

how to use

Use just-gathered basil leaves in pestos and tomato sauces, or snip them into green summer salads for a tasty surprise. Add leaves to hot water to make a tea that relieves nausea, fever, and gas pain. Use dried leaves to add a sweet perfume to potpourri. If you allow basil to set flowers, you can use the spikes for interest and aroma in fresh herbal bouquets.

OCIMUM BASILICUM

ZONES: All

TYPE: Annual

LIGHT: Full sun

SIZE: 2–3 feet tall, 1–2 feet wide

INTEREST: Intensely fragrant and delicious dark green foliage

USES: Aromatic, culinary, medicinal

SWEET MARJORAM

how to grow

Sweet marjoram likes well-drained soil in full sun. It is not drought tolerant, however, so amend the soil with plenty of compost before planting, and water when needed. Buy starter plants or sow seeds indoors early in spring. Plant outdoors 8 inches apart after the last frost. For more compact plants and more leaves, pinch the growing tips.

Of the three popular marjorams—sweet marjoram, pot marjoram, and wild marjoram—sweet marjoram is the most fragrant and delicious. It forms a low, bushy mound of ¼- to 1-inch-long gray-green oval leaves. The small white flowers appear at the stem tips from summer to fall. Knotlike bunches of gray bracts surround the blossoms, the inspiration for its other common name, knotted marjoram. Sweet marjoram, thyme, and basil are often planted together in the garden for their complementary shapes, colors, and fragrances. They are often used together in cooking.

ORIGANUM MAJORANA

ZONES: 9–10

TYPE: Perennial grown as an annual

LIGHT: Full sun

SIZE: 1–2 feet tall, 1–2 feet wide

INTEREST: Fragrant gray-green oval leaves on mounded stems tipped with knots of gray bracts

USES: Aromatic, culinary, medicinal

how to use

Well-known ingredients in Greek, German, and Italian cuisines, marjoram's flowers, leaves, stems, and seeds are all edible. They are prized for the delicate spiciness they add to meats, soups, stews, pasta, and sauces. This herb has also been used for its sedative and antiseptic properties, as well as for an aid to digestion and menstrual irregularity. Try a mellow nightcap of 2 teaspoons of fresh leaves steeped in a cup of boiling water. Sweet marjoram has also been used in perfumes, herbal baths, and sachets.

GREEK OREGANO

how to grow

Plant Greek oregano in light, well-drained soil. Let it dry out between waterings.

It is somewhat heat and drought resistant. Greek oregano's fragrance makes it a nice addition near seating areas.

Don't confuse this species with the pink-flowered *Origanum vulgare* (wild marjoram), which is invasive, as well as flavorless. The subspecies *hirtum* has an intense slightly sweet, slightly bitter flavor.

how to use

Dried or fresh Greek oregano has a variety of culinary uses—in tomato sauce, with vegetables, and with meat and fish. The flavor is more intense when the leaves are dried rather than fresh. Medicinally, the oil has been used for respiratory and digestive ailments, although its effects are not proven.

ORIGANUM VULGARE SUBSP. HIRTUM

ZONES: 5–10

TYPE: Perennial grown as an annual

LIGHT: Full sun

SIZE: 12–24 inches, 12–18 inches wide

INTEREST: Extremely fragrant foliage and small white flowers

USES: Aromatic, culinary

PASSIONFLOWER

how to grow

Passionflower likes a warm, sunny location in well-drained, sandy soil. Extra water and a little shade help it grow its best in very warm regions. In northern areas, it makes an excellent container plant that is easily overwintered indoors. Propagate from seeds in spring or cuttings in summer.

The passionflower vine climbs by wrapping tendrils around supports such as shrubs, trellises, chicken wire, and lazy gardeners. Cut it back in late winter or early spring before new growth appears. Planted in the ground, passionflower produces many suckers that should be thinned in late fall or winter. Mulch for winter protection.

Passionflower is sometimes troubled by thrips and mealybugs, as well as by cucumber mosaic virus, which mottles the foliage and stunts growth. Remove diseased plants immediately and keep the area around the plant weed-free, because some weeds serve as hosts for the virus. Spray insecticidal soap on infested plants to control insects.

Passionflower is as useful as its flowers are spectacular. Native to southern North America, passionflower bears scented 2- to 3-inch-wide summer blooms in light purple to white. The vigorous vines climb by means of curly tendrils and quickly cover fences and other supports. The medium green, deeply lobed leaves make a bitter-tasting tea that calms the nerves and relieves anxiety. When fully ripe, the fruit is sweetly aromatic and is delightful when used fresh in fruit salads.

how to use

The fruit of passionflower has many seeds embedded in its sweet, succulent pulp, which is delicious when used fresh in desserts or jams. Unfortunately, only gardeners in warm climates can enjoy the fruit, because it ripens in fall and in cold-climate gardens it cannot fully mature before being killed by frost. The stems and leaves contain sedating, nonaddictive properties, so they are often brewed into a calming tea.

PASSIFLORA INCARNATA

ZONES: 6–10

TYPE: Perennial

LIGHT: Full sun to part shade

SIZE: Vine 15–30 feet tall

INTEREST: Fragrant, showy lavender flowers followed by edible egg-sized yellow fruit

USES: Decorative, medicinal

SCENTED GERANIUM

how to grow

Scented geraniums require well-drained, evenly moist soil in full sun for maximum fragrance. If grown in small containers, water when the top of the soil is dry. If the pot is large, stick your finger at least an inch into the soil to check for dryness. Too much watering leads to soil-borne diseases and root rot, while too little turns the leaves yellow.

Fertilize with a water-soluble fertilizer at half strength every other watering during the growing season. Every fourth time you fertilize, add a teaspoon of Epsom salts to a gallon of the fertilizer solution to supply the magnesium needed by scented geraniums.

Gardeners marvel at the intense and varied fragrances of scented geraniums. Some of them—for example, lemon-scented *Pelargonium crispum*—need only a touch to release their aroma. The rich fragrance of others, such as rose-scented *P. graveolens* (pictured here), is readily apparent. Nutmeg geranium has trailing stems suitable for hanging baskets; peppermint geranium, *P. tomento-sum*, boasts fuzzy silver leaves on stems up to 4 feet tall. The variety 'Chocolate Mint' has gray-green leaves accented with brown, and it has a sweet, minty fragrance. Both of these look lovely in a pot or spilling over a retaining wall.

how to use

Although the flowers are short-lived, the foliage of this herb lives for weeks, retaining a handsome appearance and fragrance. Rose, lemon, and mint varieties add flavor to many recipes. Candy the leaves with egg white and extra-fine sugar (see page 124). Rose geraniums add flavor to sugar, jelly, cake, icing, sorbet, and herbal tea and vinegar. Dry the leaves for potpourri.

PELARGONIUM

ZONES: All

TYPE: Tender perennial grown as an annual

LIGHT: Full sun

SIZE: Variable height and width

INTEREST: Strongly scented leaves and delicate white, pink, or lavender flowers

USES: Aromatic, culinary

CURLED PARSLEY

how to grow

Parsley is easy to grow but the seeds are slow to germinate; if you'd rather not wait, buy small starter plants for your garden at a nursery instead. This herb prefers moist, well-drained soil with plenty of organic matter and a location with part shade to full sun. To boost germination, soak seeds overnight in warm water. Sow indoors 8 weeks before the last frost. Plant seedlings 8 inches apart. Start harvesting when plants are 6 or 7 inches tall, taking the older outer leaves to allow for new leaf growth in the center. A somewhat less reliable method of propagation is to let a plant go to seed in your garden and hope it will self-sow, rewarding you the following spring with numerous seedlings.

Curled parsley's crisp foliage garnishes everything from a platter of deviled eggs at a casual backyard barbecue to a slab of grilled salmon at a fancy restaurant. Parsley is a nutritious food, high in iron and vitamins A, C, and E. It's also quite tasty, adding a mild but distinctive flavor to many foods. With its divided, curly leaves crimped at the margins, this herb looks as charming edging a flower bed as it does garnishing a tray of hors d'oeuvres. The tidy plant bears flat clusters of greenish yellow flowers in its second summer, followed by small, ribbed oval seeds.

PETROSELINUM CRISPUM

ZONES: All

TYPE: Biennial grown as an annual

LIGHT: Full sun to part shade

SIZE: 1 foot tall, 1 foot wide

INTEREST: Rosettes of curly dark green leaves with flat umbels of yellowish green flowers in the second year

USES: Culinary

how to use

Parsley can be eaten fresh, dried, or frozen. Use it as a garnish or chop it and mix it with food just before serving. As a biennial, parsley flowers the second year on 3-foot stems. Its foliage tastes bitter the second year, so grow new plants each spring for a steady supply of fresh young leaves. Flat-leaved parsley has a stronger flavor and is better for cooking than the curly-leaved varieties.

COWSLIP

how to grow

Cowslip prefers full sun to part shade in spring and full shade in summer. Plant in spring in well-drained soil generously amended with organic matter, topped with mulch. Propagate cowslip by division after flowers have faded in late spring to early summer. You can also collect the ripe seeds, sowing them immediately after gathering, or let the plants self-sow. Cowslip grows particularly well in the Pacific Northwest, where the cool summers and mild winters are similar to those of England.

Remove slugs and snails by hand, and aphids and spider mites by spraying with water or insecticidal soap.

Cowslip is an attractive low-growing perennial wildflower of England and continental Europe that has become a popular addition to North American gardens. The plant forms a basal rosette of soft, crinkled, ovate gray-green leaves. In early spring, downy 6-inch stems rise from the center, topped by umbels of deep yellow, slightly nodding flowers. The fragrant blooms have orange-spotted throats surrounded by five petals. Cowslip is charming at the edge of a shady path or border, or in masses in woodland gardens or rockeries.

how to use

Cowslip flowers are rich in sweet nectar—a treat to people, butterflies, and hummingbirds alike. Sprinkle fresh blossoms in salads for a colorful touch, or brew the fresh or dried flowers into a calming tea to soothe headaches and calm nerves. Cowslip is a traditional ingredient in syrups, vinegars, and country wines.

PRIMULA VERIS

ZONES: 5–8

TYPE: Perennial

LIGHT: Sun in spring, shade in summer

SIZE: 6 inches tall, 6 inches wide

INTEREST: Fragrant yellow flowers and rich green, oblong leaves

USES: Culinary, decorative, medicinal

APOTHECARY ROSE

how to grow

Apothecary rose needs full sun to ensure maximum bloom. Plant in early spring or fall in a sheltered location with plenty of morning sun to dry the dew from the leaves. In southern areas, some light afternoon shade protects the plants from extreme heat. Soil should be slightly acidic, very well drained, and contain plenty of organic matter.

For grafted plants, set the bud union 2 inches below the soil surface in cold climates and at ground level in warm areas. Fertilize apothecary rose once in early spring with dehydrated cow manure and bonemeal, or use a commercial fertilizer for roses. Regular, generous watering early in the day and good air circulation help prevent powdery mildew and black spot on the leaves. If aphids appear, spray with insecticidal soap.

Apothecary rose combines beauty and delicious scent with winter hardiness and disease resistance to make it a must-grow plant in the flower border or herb garden. It flowers heavily for 4 to 5 weeks in summer, producing fragrant semidouble blooms in deep pink with gold stamens, followed by round red fruit (hips) in fall. It freely suckers when grown on its own roots, making it suitable for planting on banks as a ground cover. You can purchase grafted plants that do not produce suckers. These plants mature into attractive 3- to 4-foot compact shrubs.

how to use

Apothecary rose was used to treat everything from colds and infections to skin problems and depression. Herbalists claim rose water or rose oil (attar of roses) in skin-care products soothes the skin; aromatherapists believe that the fragrance relieves anxiety. It's also a beautiful cut flower, with a lovely floral fragrance that quickly fills a room. When dried, the petals are an excellent choice for conserves and potpourris. Add fresh petals to salads, candy them (see page 124), or use in syrups and jellies.

ROSA GALLICA VAR. OFFICINALIS

ZONES: 3–8

TYPE: Perennial shrub

LIGHT: Full sun

SIZE: 3 feet tall, 3 feet wide

INTEREST: Fragrant, semidouble deep pink flowers with gold stamens; crinkled, medium green leaves

USES: Aromatic, culinary, decorative, medicinal

ROSEMARY

how to grow

Rosemary grows best in well-drained, slightly moist soil. Set plants about 2 feet apart for an upright hedge, or use the prostrate form, also spaced 2 feet apart, to create a fragrant ground cover. To keep plants compact, cut back after blooming. You can also pinch the growing tips to promote bushiness.

Grow rosemary from seeds or take stem cuttings from new wood in spring and remove the bottom leaves. Place the cuttings in damp sand or water until roots appear. When planted outdoors, rosemary is pest-free. Indoors, it is susceptible to houseplant pests such as aphids, mealybugs, and spider mites. To combat these, spray the plants regularly with a weak solution of Murphy's Oil Soap and water.

Rosemary, with its needlelike leaves and potent fragrance, is one of the most useful and versatile herbs. As a kitchen seasoning, the leaves are used for flavoring many recipes. In mild climates, it can grow to 4 feet tall; in cooler climates, where it is treated as an annual or wintered indoors, it tends to be smaller. Its thick foliage can be shaped into a formal hedge or a standard, a slender trunk topped with a sphere of evergreen foliage. Rosemary begins blooming in late winter on old wood and continues into spring with two-lipped flowers in shades of pale blue, lilac, and white.

how to use

The intense, resinous flavor of rosemary tastes delicious with meat, chicken, seafood, vegetables, soups, breads, and sauces. Use whole sprigs (remove before serving) as a light accent to recipes, or try minced fresh leaves for a more robust flavor. Rosemary tea may make you sleepy. To brew it, steep 1 teaspoon of dried rosemary or 3 teaspoons of fresh flowers and leaves per cup of boiling water. Herbalists say that rosemary eases gas pains and headaches, aids eyesight and memory, and helps keep hair and complexion healthy.

ROSMARINUS OFFICINALIS

ZONES: 8–10

TYPE: Perennial sometimes grown as an annual

LIGHT: Full sun

SIZE: 1–4 feet tall, 1–4 feet wide

INTEREST: Fragrant, evergreen foliage and blue to white flowers that attract bees

USES: Aromatic, culinary, decorative, medicinal

FRENCH SORREL

how to grow

Plant seeds in the spring, and watch them grow! Quick to germinate, French sorrel can grow in light to heavy soils but prefers it to be moist and well drained, though it can tolerate drought.

French sorrel can be harvested young, when the leaves have a mild taste, or later, when the flavor becomes more intense and tangy.

RUMEX SCUTATUS

ZONES: 5–10

TYPE: Perennial

LIGHT: Full sun to partial shade

SIZE: 2 feet tall

INTEREST: Fragrant foliage

USES: Culinary

how to use

Use the tangy, citrusy leaves to flavor meat, fish, and eggs. The leaves can keep for 1 or 2 weeks refrigerated, and they can be frozen to use later. Raw leaves are a good addition to salads.

PINEAPPLE SAGE

how to grow

Though it will tolerate some shade, poor soil, and some drought, pineapple sage grows most successfully in full sun and evenly moist soil. Plant it where you want to attract hummingbirds and butterflies. Propagate by planting rooted cuttings in pots, overwintering them indoors in a sunny spot, and then planting in the garden in spring. It can also be propagated by seeds or layering.

With its pretty bright red flowers, pineapple sage is named for the aroma and taste of pineapple when its leaves are crushed. A member of the mint family, it is native to the mountains of Mexico and Guatemala.

how to use

Use the bright red edible flowers in salads and as a garnish to impart a minty, lemony flavor. Use the tangy, pineapple-flavored leaves to dress up drinks. Use the smaller, more tender leaves for more flavor. Used in a tea, pineapple sage may help reduce anxiety and nausea.

SALVIA ELEGANS

ZONES: 8–10

TYPE: Perennial grown as an annual

LIGHT: Full sun

SIZE: 3–4 feet tall, 2–3 feet wide

INTEREST: Showy red flowers in late summer and fall, and fragrant leaves

USES: Aromatic, culinary

CULINARY SAGE

how to grow

Native to the Mediterranean and North Africa, sage can tolerate poor soil but needs good drainage to thrive, a trait that makes it excellent for containers and raised beds. It is prone to root rot in wet conditions.

In warm climates, sage is evergreen; in cold areas, the plants die back in winter and need spring pruning for healthy new growth. Divide garden sage every few years, and replace it when the stems grow both hard and woody. Plant rooted cuttings in pots and overwinter indoors on a sunny windowsill.

Sage, a member of the mint family, is a beautiful plant with downy, wrinkled gray-green leaves. It is graced with blue-purple summertime flowers. The blossoms, which attract bees, are two-lipped and grow in four to eight false whorls at axils along the stem tips. The long-stemmed leaves hang gracefully from the stems and have a spicy aroma. Ancient herbalists believed that eating the herb could slow the aging process and sharpen the memory. Sage, which means "wise," has become a symbol of wisdom and immortality.

SALVIA OFFICINALIS

ZONES: 5–8

TYPE: Perennial

LIGHT: Full sun

SIZE: 2 feet tall, 2 feet wide

INTEREST: Soft, fragrant gray-green leaves and blue-purple flowers

USES: Aromatic, culinary, decorative, medicinal

how to use

The appealing, slightly musky taste of sage leaves adds flavorful depth to meat, poultry, fish, soups, and many vegetables. Sage also makes fatty meats more digestible. For the strongest flavor, cook with dried leaves. To prepare sage for use as a seasoning, grind fresh leaves in a food mill or rub dried leaves through a fine screen. The crushed dried leaves make a refreshing tea.

SUMMER SAVORY

how to grow

Sun-loving summer savory needs dry, sandy soil with excellent drainage. You can grow this annual equally well indoors in a container or outdoors in the garden. Propagate from cuttings or seeds. Sow the seeds, which germinate quickly, either indoors in flats 4 to 6 weeks before the last frost or directly in the garden where you want the plants to grow. Thin seedlings so they are 6 to 10 inches apart.

The narrow green leaves of summer savory resemble rosemary but have a tangy flavor all their own. Ancient herbalists attributed increased sex drive to summer savory (and the opposite to winter savory). Today, the reputation of summer savory lies with its peppery taste, which adds delicate spiciness to many meat and vegetable dishes. The plant forms a relaxed mound of slender, hairy, 12- to 18-inch-tall stems covered with narrow gray-green leaves. A member of the mint family, savory bears small groups of white or lilac flowers in the upper leaf axils. The blossoms, leaves, and stems are all aromatic. The botanical name, *Satureja,* derives from the Greek word for "satyr" and refers to the herb's old-time use as an aphrodisiac.

how to use

Summer savory tastes good both fresh and dried, served with beans and vegetables, and in herb butters, vinegars, soups, and teas. It makes a quite pleasant digestive tea, which can also relieve diarrhea. The flavor of summer savory is strongest just before the plant begins to flower, so that is a good time to harvest it.

SATUREJA HORTENSIS

ZONES: All

TYPE: Annual

LIGHT: Full sun

SIZE: 1–2 feet tall, 1–2 feet wide

INTEREST: Scented, narrow, pointed leaves and two-lipped lilac or white flowers that attract bees

USES: Culinary, medicinal

WINTER SAVORY

how to grow

Grow winter savory in well-drained soil and don't overwater, as water-logged roots can rot. It is even a bit drought tolerant. Prune plants in early spring before they break dormancy. Harvest the leaves just before the plants flower.

Grown on rocky, hot Mediterranean mountainsides, where it is native, winter savory forms a low, 1-foot-tall and 2-foot-wide mound of shiny evergreen leaves. Abundant whorls of small white, lavender, or pink flowers attract bees in late summer.

SATUREJA MONTANA

ZONES: 6–8

TYPE: Perennial grown as an annual

LIGHT: Full sun to partial shade

SIZE: 6–12 inches tall, 12–18 inches wide

INTEREST: White to light purple flowers in midsummer

USES: Culinary, medicinal

how to use

The leaves—which can be used fresh or dried, raw or cooked—have a peppery flavor that is more intense than that of summer savory. Medicinally, it is said to aid a variety of digestive ailments when ingested. It can also be used topically to relieve the pain of insect stings.

STEVIA

how to grow

Grow stevia in rich and moist well-drained soil. Roots can rot if they stay too wet, so be careful not to overwater. In climates colder than Zone 10, containers are a good option, as they can be brought inside to overwinter before the first frost. In warmer zones, partial shade will help.

Also known as sweetleaf, stevia has leaves that are nearly 300 times as sweet as sugar. A member of the aster family, stevia is native to northern South America. It is used in many countries as a sweetener, though in the United States it is classified as an herbal supplement and is not approved for use as a food additive.

how to use

Dry the leaves and grind them up to use as a sweetener. Or use fresh leaves in drinks, such as tea. (The leaves are sweeter when dried than when fresh.) Use approximately one-quarter to one-eighth the amount of dried stevia as you would sugar. Anyone with diabetes or low blood pressure should use stevia with caution, as it can lower blood pressure and cause hypoglycemic symptoms.

STEVIA REBAUDIANA

ZONES: 10–11

TYPE: Perennial grown as an annual

LIGHT: Full sun to partial shade

SIZE: 1–2 feet tall, 1–2 feet wide

INTEREST: Showy white flowers that bloom in late summer

USES: Culinary

MEXICAN MINT MARIGOLD

how to grow

Mexican mint marigold needs a long, hot growing season and plenty of sun to bloom its best. Pinch the growing tips for a fuller plant. In northern areas, plant seeds 6 weeks before the last frost. From Zone 9 south, sow seeds outdoors anytime. Set plants 1 foot apart. Mexican mint marigold is pest- and disease-free.

A rich licorice aroma permeates the leaves, stems, and flowers of Mexican mint marigold. The plant has erect stems and narrow, lance-shaped leaves about ¾ inch long. Mexican mint marigold bears single deep yellow blooms at the ends of the stems. In colder climates, where it is grown as an annual for its fragrant foliage, it develops few flowers. In hot climates, it is a good substitute for French tarragon.

TAGETES LUCIDA

ZONES: 8–10

TYPE: Perennial grown as an annual

LIGHT: Full sun to part shade

SIZE: 3 feet tall, 3 feet wide

INTEREST: Bushy clump of aromatic foliage and single, yellow flowers

USES: Aromatic, culinary

how to use

Mexican mint marigold tea contains vitamin C and phosphorus and is used as a nutritious tonic. Brew it from the petals alone or from whole dried flowers and leaves. Add dried flowers and leaves to potpourris, or use them fresh or dried in cooking as a substitute for French tarragon. Mexican mint marigold may help improve digestion, lower fevers, and relieve anxiety. When burned, the plant's aroma repels insects. Applied to skin, it works as a tick remover.

THYME

how to grow

Thyme grows best in full sun and light, well-drained soil. This pest-free Mediterranean native tolerates heat and drought, but it does poorly in wet soil or shade. A southern exposure or raised bed provides the most favorable growing conditions. Keep areas around plants weeded, and mulch with a nonabsorbent mulch such as sand or gravel to inhibit disease. Overwinter plants beneath a blanket of pine branches. Cut back in early spring to remove woody stems, and after flowering to stimulate growth and prevent self-seeding. Pinch back stems to encourage a bushier habit. Propagate from seeds or cuttings or by division.

Highly acclaimed for its strong, pungent taste, garden thyme enhances the flavor of meats, breads, and vegetables. Of all the thymes, this is the most flavorful. It has an upright habit with pink to lilac flowers in the axils of the stem tips. A highly respected member of the mint family, it looks and smells delightful in herbal wreaths. Thyme makes an attractive edging or ground cover in the herb garden. Planted throughout a vegetable garden, it may repel pests such as cabbage worms. Bees make flavorful honey from its summertime flowers.

how to use

Thyme leaves taste stronger dried than fresh. Thyme is a basic component in a *bouquet garni*, along with parsley, sweet bay, rosemary, and other herbs. Use it with meats, fish, eggs, and vegetables and in sauces, stews, soups, gumbos, and breads. Thyme tea may prevent nightmares and soothe headaches and hangovers. Syrup made of thyme and honey is good for sore throats and colds.

THYMUS VULGARIS

ZONES: 4–9

TYPE: Perennial

LIGHT: Full sun

SIZE: 12 inches tall, 8 inches wide

INTEREST: Aromatic gray-green leaves and lilac flowers that attract bees

USES: Culinary, decorative, medicinal

NASTURTIUM

how to grow

Nasturtium is easy to please and thrives in ordinary soil with regular watering. Do not fertilize—in rich soil you will get more leaves than flowers. Nasturtium tolerates both partial shade and full sun. Plant the seeds 6 to 12 inches apart and cover with ½ inch of soil. Nasturtium seeds germinate quickly and the plants spread fast but are not invasive. Although subject to aphids, nasturtium is otherwise pest-free. It may self-sow, but seedlings can be lifted easily and moved to another location.

Nasturtiums taste as good as they look. The showy leaves and colorful flowers have a sharp, peppery flavor similar to watercress. The flat, rounded leaves have an attractive, radiating pattern of light green veins. Nasturtiums grow fast and are easy to propagate and maintain. The seeds are large, making them ideal for children to plant. The cheery plants look wonderful covering a bank, spilling over a stone wall, tied to a trellis, or climbing a garden fence. Wherever you grow nasturtium, you won't be disappointed. It adds a wonderful splash of color and peppery taste to many dishes.

TROPAEOLUM MAJUS

ZONES: All

TYPE: Annual

LIGHT: Full sun to part shade

SIZE: 1 foot tall, 2 feet wide

INTEREST: Round leaves and cheerful red, orange, yellow, or bicolor flowers

USES: Culinary, decorative

how to use

The leaves, flowers, and seeds of nasturtiums are high in vitamin C and useful in cooking and medicine. Flowers, buds, and leaves add spiciness and beauty to salads. As an hors d'oeuvre or luncheon dish, the flowers look and taste delicious stuffed with a blend of cream cheese and minced nasturtium leaves. Leaves also enhance cheese and egg dishes. The unripened seeds can be pickled and used as a substitute for capers.

GARDEN HELIOTROPE
VALERIANA
OFFICINALIS

ZONES: 3–9

TYPE: Perennial

LIGHT: Full sun

SIZE: 3–5 feet tall, 4 feet wide

INTEREST: Pink, white, or lavender flowers in fragrant 4-inch-wide clusters

USES: Aromatic, decorative, medicinal

VALERIAN

how to grow

Valerian thrives in rich, moist, well-drained soil in full sun. It tolerates both acidic and alkaline soils. Propagate from seeds in spring, covering seeds lightly with soil. (The germination rate may be as low as 50 percent of the seeds planted.) Propagate by dividing plants every 3 years in spring from Zone 6 north, and fall from Zone 7 south. Valerian rhizomes spread quickly, forming new plants, which can be lifted and moved elsewhere in the garden. If older clumps have begun to decline, invigorate the plants by dividing.

This fleshy herb, a favorite selection in old-fashioned gardens, forms an attractive clump of basal leaves, topped by tall stems with 2- to 4-inch flower clusters. Gardeners enjoy the sweet fragrance of valerian's pink, white, or lavender flowers. Valerian's aromatic roots drive felines wild but have a sedative effect on people. Oil extracted from valerian roots is used to season tobacco and add flavor to liqueurs, beers, and soft drinks. This herb works well at the back of perennial borders, in rock gardens, or when naturalized as part of a wildflower meadow. The leaves are divided into seven to ten leaflet pairs. While the sweet scent of valerian flowers is reminiscent of heliotrope (thus the common name, garden heliotrope), the rest of the plant, especially the roots, is somewhat malodorous, smelling like old socks to most people.

how to use

An effective tranquilizer, valerian is a popular over-the-counter remedy in Europe. Valerian tea calms the mind and alleviates insomnia, nervous headaches, and upset stomachs. The tea, which tastes bitter but is soothing, is best brewed from fall-harvested rhizomes; use ½ teaspoon of dried ground root per cup of boiling water. Sweeten the tea with honey or sugar for improved flavor. Valerian in bathwater may have a soothing effect.

CAUTION: While a little valerian (a cup of tea per day) may be helpful, more may be toxic. In large quantities, valerian may cause agitation, headaches, and stupor.

FLANNEL MULLEIN

how to grow

Flannel mullein grows best in poor, dry, well-drained soil in full sun. Propagate from seeds in spring or fall, or from root cuttings in late winter or spring. If you prefer a mass planting rather than a single specimen, set the plants about 2 to 3 feet apart. In its first year, flannel mullein grows a basal rosette of gray-green leaves. The next year, its flower stem rises up to 6 feet. If the stalk is not cut back after blooming, it may self-sow prolifically, producing large crops of easily transplanted seedlings. The soft, feltlike leaves may be subject to caterpillar attack, and in dry climates they get dusty and look a little worn out by summer's end.

Whether in the garden or by the road, flannel mullein has a presence few plants can challenge. Its towering height lends architectural interest and its dramatic appearance gives it enormous visual power, making it an excellent choice as an accent plant. Mullein produces a basal rosette of 6- to 9-inch-long felted gray-green leaves from which rises a strong 6-foot-tall flower stalk. The woolly stem leaves are smaller and lead to a long flower spike studded with five-petaled yellow flowers 1 inch in length.

VERBASCUM THAPSUS

ZONES: 5–9

TYPE: Biennial

LIGHT: Full sun

SIZE: 2–6 feet tall, 2 feet wide

INTEREST: Tall spike of yellow flowers with a rosette of velvety gray-green leaves

USES: Decorative, medicinal

how to use

Mullein looks terrific in groups at the back of a sunny border. A single plant makes a strong impact in front. Because it thrives in dry conditions, it also does well on slopes. A tea made with 1 teaspoon dried or 3 teaspoons fresh leaves or flowers steeped in 1 cup boiling water may help lung problems and act as a mild tranquilizer and pain reliever. (Tea from the leaves has a pungent taste, while flower tea is sweet.)

CAUTION: Do not ingest any mullein tea or decoction without first straining it to remove the downy hairs, which can irritate the throat.

VIOLA ODORATA

ZONES: 4–9

TYPE: Perennial

LIGHT: Full sun to shade, depending on climate

SIZE: 4–6 inches tall, 12 inches wide

INTEREST: Fragrant flowers in purple, white, or lavender with dark green heart-shaped leaves

USES: Culinary, decorative, medicinal

SWEET VIOLET

how to grow

To encourage full, lavish clumps of lovely foliage, grow violets in part shade in rich, moist, humus-rich soil amended with plenty of compost. If you really favor the flowers, play tough with your violets by providing drier and less fertile accommodations. Cutting back clumps in fall ensures a handsome fresh mound of foliage in spring. Propagate from seeds or by division in the spring. If planted near a lawn, sweet violet will spread into it. It also makes a good ground cover.

One of about five hundred species of violas, sweet violet is especially appreciated for its beauty, sweet scent, and association with love. The plant is as useful as it is romantic and beautiful. The flowers and leaves can be used in everything from salads to medicinal teas and fragrant bouquets. The cheerful blossoms are nice additions to herb gardens or along perennial borders. The heart-shaped leaves are dark green with toothed margins. A tuft of violets sends out runners that in turn become new rooted clumps. Moreover, sweet violets also self-sow, resulting in new seedlings each spring.

how to use

Violets make pretty, sweet-smelling cut flowers for nosegays and strewing. Harvest the flowers when first open, remove the stems, and enjoy them fresh or dry them for later use. Add fresh flowers to fruit and green salads, float them in drinks and punch bowls, or candy them for dessert decorations (see page 124). Dry in warm, dry shade to preserve their color and, for a short time, their fragrance for potpourris and flower crafts. Make a medicinal, calming tea from flowers or the leaves. A compress of crushed leaves may reduce swelling, while the roots and flowers have a cleansing, laxative effect. The violet-colored flowers also yield a purple dye.

YUCCA

how to grow

This slow-growing adaptable plant, a member of the agave family, thrives in poor, dry soil and tolerates cold winters, hot and humid summers, and windy conditions. Native to the semidesert areas of the southwestern United States, through the Southeast, and along the Atlantic coast from Rhode Island to Mexico, yucca needs well-drained soil. The only place it doesn't do well is a wet, shady site.

Propagate from root cuttings or by separating rooted offsets from the base of the plant and transplanting them to new locations. Remove old flower stalks and dead leaves before new growth begins in spring.

Yucca's bold, sword-shaped evergreen leaves are 1 to 2 inches wide and 2 to 3 feet long, with sharp points and curly threads along the edges. The tall central flower stem has a panicle of white, waxy, drooping flowers, each measuring 2 to 3 inches across. The flowers, which have six petals and six stamens, are followed by large, woody pods suitable for dried flower arrangements. Yucca spreads slowly by offshoots consisting of similar rosettes with the characteristic sword-shaped leaves. It looks outstanding massed in an arid garden or used singly as a focal point in a flower bed or border.

how to use

In the landscape, yucca's architectural quality harmonizes with diverse settings ranging from building foundations to perennial gardens and grassy or rocky banks. With its evergreen foliage and dramatic flower stalk, yucca is stunning as a container plant. Like Native Americans, you can use yucca's sturdy, pliant fibers to weave baskets, or double-boil the shoots to make a stimulating tonic. Mashing the roots in water releases the natural saponins (lathering agents) to make homemade soap or shampoo. Collect yucca's large, woody fruit pods in fall for dried flower arrangements.

YUCCA
FILAMENTOSA

ZONES: 5–10

TYPE: Perennial

LIGHT: Full sun

SIZE: 2–3 feet tall (foliage);
5–6 feet tall (flowers);
5–6 feet wide

INTEREST: Stiff, swordlike
foliage with an upright
branched spike of large,
white bell-shaped flowers

USES: Decorative,
medicinal

HARVESTING *AND* PRESERVING HERBS

when to harvest

Harvesting herbs is not a difficult thing to do. A snip here and there yields plenty of basil, thyme, and many other herbs. The trick to harvesting is not so much the method as the timing. Many herbs rely on volatile oils for their flavor and aroma; the concentrations of these oils change over time. To harvest the best-tasting herbs, you must gather them when the oils are at their peak. Oil content changes over the course of the growing season as well as over the course of each day.

As a general rule, herbs grown for their leaves, such as basil and rosemary, are most potent from the time flower buds form to when the buds begin to open. Biennial herbs, including parsley, are best before any flower stalk appears. Harvest leafy herbs in the morning when the leaves are dry but before they are in direct sunlight.

Flowers, such as daylilies and violets, are most flavorful when the blossoms are about three-quarters open. Herbs grown for their roots, such as purple coneflower, are most potent in fall after the plant has flowered and finished its yearly growth.

PRESERVING HERBS BY DRYING

There are many methods of drying herbs, ranging from ancient to high-tech. All are worth a try, depending on your needs and facilities. Some preserve more flavor and color than others.

AIR DRYING

Air drying is an ancient method of preserving herbs and is a good method for preparing large amounts of leaves. To air-dry, gather the herb into bunches of five to seven stems each. Tie the bunches with twine or string and hang them upside down in a warm, dimly lit room. Leave enough space between bundles so the herbs do not touch. If the air is humid, use a fan to increase air circulation and reduce the chance of mold forming on the leaves. Check the plants frequently. When dry, crumble them and store in lidded glass jars in a cool, dimly lit place.

Air drying is easy to do and an excellent method of preparing plants for dried arrangements. The herbs do lose some flavor, and plants left hanging too long can become moldy, dusty, or tasteless.

OVEN DRYING

Oven drying is an option for drying herbs where space is limited. Spread the leaves or roots in a single layer on a cookie sheet and place in the oven. The pilot light on gas ovens provides just enough heat to dry the herbs slowly and evenly. Fluff the herbs once or twice a day while they dry—usually for a period of 3 to 5 days. If using an electric oven, set it on warm and leave the door ajar. Check herbs daily, turning the oven off at night and resetting in the morning—until the herbs are dry. Oven drying is satisfactory for small amounts of herbs but can rob the leaves of flavor. It also is not energy-efficient. This method is excellent for preparing roots, however.

COOL-AIR DRYING

Cool-air drying is another name for refrigerator drying, a technique that has become very popular over the last few years. It produces very high-quality results and retains excellent flavor and color. Cool-air drying can be done only in frost-free refrigerators. It works best for leaves, flower petals, and herbs that lose flavor quickly, such as dill and parsley. To cool-air dry herbs, lay paper towels on a cookie sheet. Spread a single layer of the herb on the paper towels and place in the refrigerator. If space is at a premium, place the herbs in an onion bag. Hang the bag from a magnetic hook attached to the inside of the refrigerator. Check the herbs daily for dryness, as drying can take anywhere from 3 days to a full week. Store the dried herbs in lidded glass jars.

Cool-air drying is useful for preparing small quantities of herbs. It does not work in crisper bins. (In theory, this technique should work well in frost-free freezers as well as frost-free refrigerators, but it doesn't.)

MICROWAVE DRYING

Microwave drying takes only brief amounts of time to produce a high-quality product. This method does require frequent monitoring, and only small amounts of an herb can be dried at any one time. Place a layer of paper towels on a microwave-safe plate. After gathering the herb, spread the leaves in a single layer on the plate. Be sure the leaves are dry and free of all surface moisture; wet leaves will cook instead of dry. Microwave on high for 1 to 3 minutes, checking the plants after each minute. The herb is "done" when the leaves feel dry to the touch and have not lost any color. The plate also heats up during this process and must cool down before being reused. Allow the herb to cool. Store in an airtight glass jar.

DEHYDRATOR DRYING

Electric dehydrators are designed to dry food by circulating heated (105° to 115°F) air over and around the food. Most manufacturers supply directions for drying herbs, which eliminates a great deal of experimentation. Most herbs dried in a dehydrator retain good flavor and color. Some, such as basil, lose too much flavor using this method. Knowing which herbs to dry in a dehydrator and which to process in other ways does require a bit of experimentation. An advantage to dehydrator drying is that the herbs do not require monitoring; just turn on the unit and wait. Dehydrators are not large appliances, so the amount of herbs you can dry in each batch is limited.

FREEZING HERBS

Freezing herbs is fast and easy, but it is not a good method for everything. Freezing damages the cells of plants, and as a result, frozen herbs often become soft and mushy when thawed. This does not matter if the herbs are used in cooking, but do not expect frozen herbs to make a good garnish. Some herbs have a nasty habit of turning black in the freezer; preserve these by drying or pureeing and then freezing. The puree will not turn black. The best herbs to freeze include dill, mint, and rosemary.

To freeze herbs, spread individual sprigs on a small tray or aluminum pie plate and place in the freezer overnight. The next day, remove the herbs and store in labeled freezer bags. Refreeze. Remove individual sprigs or leaves as you need them. Reseal and return the bag to the freezer.

GLOSSARY

ACIDIC SOIL: Soil with a pH value of less than 7.0.

ALBA: A type of old garden rose typically bearing clusters of small, fragrant white flowers.

ALKALINE SOIL: Soil with a pH value of more than 7.0.

ANNUAL: A plant that completes its life cycle (germination, flowering, seed production, and death) in one growing season.

AXIL: The notchlike angle formed by the union of the leaf stem (petiole) and the plant stem.

BASAL LEAF: A leaf that grows from the base of a plant.

BASAL ROSETTE: A cluster of leaves at the base of a plant.

BIENNIAL: A plant that completes its life cycle (germination, flowering, seed production, and death) in two growing seasons.

BLACK SPOT: A fungal disease that infects many types of roses, causing black spots to form on leaves and ultimately leaves falling from the plant (defoliation). The disease is most severe during wet, warm weather.

BLADE: The broad, flat portion of a leaf.

BOLTING: The rapid growth of a flower stalk; usually refers to annuals and biennials.

BONEMEAL: Ground raw or steamed bone that is added to the soil as a phosphorous-rich fertilizer.

BOURBON: A type of old garden rose with stout, compact habit.

BRACT: Leaves at the base of a flower that are different in shape, form, or texture from other leaves on the plant.

BUD BREAK: When a dormant bud begins to elongate and grow.

BUD EYE: A dormant bud in the axil of a leaf. Bud eyes are used in a form of rose propagation called bud grafting.

BUD UNION: The junction between the understock and the grafted variety above it.

CANE: A long, often unbranched woody stem.

CENTIFOLIA: A type of old garden rose, also called the cabbage rose, similar in appearance to the gallica rose.

CHLOROSIS: The reduction of chlorophyll in a leaf, resulting in a yellowish appearance. Chlorosis can have many causes, including nutrient deficiencies and disease.

COMPOUND LEAF: A leaf with two or more leaflets attached to the central leaf stalk.

CROWN: The region of the bud union near the soil line where the understock and the grafted variety are joined.

CROWN BORER: An insect that tunnels into shoots and stems to lay eggs. The emerging larvae then feed on the surrounding healthy plant tissue.

CULTIVAR: A variety of plant that has persisted through cultivation and been given a name. An example of a cultivar is the rose 'New Dawn'.

CUTTING: A plant portion that is removed from the parent plant and treated to regrow stems, roots, or leaves to become a self-sustaining plant.

DAMASK: A type of old garden rose cultivated at least since the time of the Crusades. Most bloom once, though some repeat in late summer.

DEADHEADING: The removal of spent flowers to encourage additional flower bud formation or discourage seed formation.

DECIDUOUS: Describing a plant that sheds all its leaves at some time during the year.

DISK FLOWER: The round, central portion of a daisy-like flower, composed of many very small, tubular flowers.

DIVISION: Propagation achieved by cutting one clump of a plant into smaller pieces that then become individual plants. Also, a new plant that has been created by this method.

DOUBLE BLOSSOM/DOUBLE FLOWER: A blossom with more petals than normal.

EVERGREEN: Describing a plant that does not shed its leaves at any time during the year. Also, a plant having this characteristic.

EVERLASTING: A plant or flower, such as curry plant, that retains much of its color and form after being gathered and dried.

FAMILY: A group of closely related genera, such as grasses or legumes.

FLORIBUNDA: A class of modern rose derived from crossing hybrid polyantha and hybrid tea roses. The flowers resemble hybrid teas in form and color, but are smaller and borne in clusters.

FOUNDATION PLANTING: Planting along the foundation or base of a building to conceal or camouflage it.

FUNGICIDE: A substance that inhibits the growth of or kills specific fungi.

GALLICA: An ancient type of old garden rose, usually with rich fragrance and colors ranging from pink to red.

GENUS: A group of closely related species. (Plural: genera)

GLAUCOUS: Having a powdery coating or a grayish color.

GRAFT: A method of propagation in which a shoot of one plant is removed and joined to another plant, called a rootstock or stock.

HABIT: A plant's distinctive, natural shape, such as spreading or conical.

HIP: The vitamin C–rich fruit of a rose.

HUMUS: Soil portion composed of partially decomposed organic matter. You can purchase or create humus to add to soil.

INSECTICIDAL SOAP: A combination of sodium or potassium salts and oils usually derived from vegetable sources. They are used to control soft-bodied insects and mites, but are largely ineffective against other insects such as beetles, wasps, and flies.

JAPANESE BEETLE: A beetle about ½ inch long with copper-brown wing covers and a metallic green head and prothorax (upper portion of body).

KEEL: A raised ridge along a portion of a plant, such as a leaf, flower, fruit, or stem.

LATERAL: A stem or flower that rises from the side of a larger stem.

LEAFLET: One of the divisions of a compound leaf.

LOPPERS: A pruning tool with long handles and a cutting blade used to trim stems and branches that are 1 to 2 inches in diameter.

MARGIN: The edge of a leaf.

MILDEW: A fungal disease. The mildew that attacks roses is most often a type of powdery mildew that begins with a curling of the leaves. As the infection advances, a white powdery coating appears on the leaves, on the buds, and near thorns on the canes.

MINIATURE: A group of roses usually less than 18 inches tall with smaller-than-normal leaves and flowers.

NODE: The points along the stem where buds develop, singly or in groups.

OBOVATE: A leaf whose blade is broader above the center. The opposite of ovate.

ORGANIC MATTER: Material derived from decomposed remains of plants and animals; includes manure and leaves.

OVATE: A leaf whose blade is broader below the center.

OWN-ROOT ROSE: A rose that has not been grafted and therefore is growing on its own roots rather than on those of another.

PANICLE: An open, usually pyramidal, cluster of flowers.

PERENNIAL: A plant that survives for 3 or more years.

PETIOLE: The stalk that attaches the leaf to the stem of a plant.

PH: The scale used to measure the concentration of hydrogen ions in a solution, which controls how acidic or alkaline the solution is. The pH scale runs from 0 to 14, with 7.0 being neutral. Any value less than 7.0 is acidic and any value exceeding 7.0 is alkaline. In horticulture, pH most often refers to the measure of soil acidity.

PINNATE: Having leaflets arranged in two rows along a central leaf stalk.

POLYANTHA: A group of hardy old garden rose hybrids with a dwarf habit and small flowers.

PROPAGATION: The technique of producing more plants.

QUARTERED: A rose blossom with three, four, or five radial segments.

RAY FLOWER: The petal-like portion arranged symmetrically around a central disk of a composite flower, such as a daisy.

RECURRENT BLOOM: Blooming periodically throughout the growing season.

REPEAT-BLOOMING ROSE: Any rose that has a nonblooming period between its spring and fall flowering periods.

RHIZOME: A horizontal underground stem that is sometimes thin, as in mint, and sometimes enlarged, as in iris, to serve as a storage organ for starches and other carbohydrates—an energy source for spring sprouting.

ROSETTE: A cluster of leaves.

RUGOSA: A group of hardy, disease-resistant hybrids derived from the beach rose (*Rosa rugosa*), with textured glossy leaves and bristly thorns along the canes.

RUNNER: A slender aboveground stem that produces a new plant at its terminal end.

RUST, ROSE: A fungal disease that manifests as bright orange dots on the undersides of leaves with yellow dots on the tops of leaves. The disease is most prevalent during moist, warm, but not hot weather. It sometimes occurs in the Northeast but is most severe in the Pacific Northwest and during winter in southern California.

SCAPE: A leafless flower stalk that rises from the ground, as in daylilies.

SEMIDOUBLE: A blossom with more than the normal number of petals but less than twice as many. In roses, a blossom with twelve to twenty-four petals.

SINGLE FLOWER: A flower with the normal number of petals for its species.

SPECIES: A group of very closely related plants.

SPORT: A genetic mutation in a developing bud that gives rise to a branch that is notably different from the rest of the plant. Many varieties began as sports that were then propagated.

STAMEN: The male portion of a flower, consisting of the filament and the anther, which contains the pollen.

STOCK: The parent plant from which propagation material, such as cuttings, is taken.

STRATIFYING: Placing seeds in a moist, cold environment for a predetermined period to satisfy the dormancy requirement in order to grow.

SUCKER: A shoot that rises from buds along the roots. As these shoots grow, they form their own roots. Suckers can then be separated from the parent plant and transplanted.

TAPROOT: The long, usually thick root grown by some plants, such as carrots. Taproots often serve as storage organs and have few branching roots. Many plants that produce taproots are difficult to transplant.

TOOTHED: Having small lobes along the margins of leaves, flowers, or other parts of a plant.

TWO-LIPPED: Divided into upper and lower sections, usually in reference to the flowers of plants in the mint family.

UMBEL: A flower cluster with floral stems that radiate from a central point, as in dill.

VARIEGATED: Having streaked or blotched coloration, other than green, on plant parts such as leaves or flowers; caused by cellular mutations that disrupt the normal production of chlorophyll.

WHORL: A group of three or more leaves that rise from a single node.

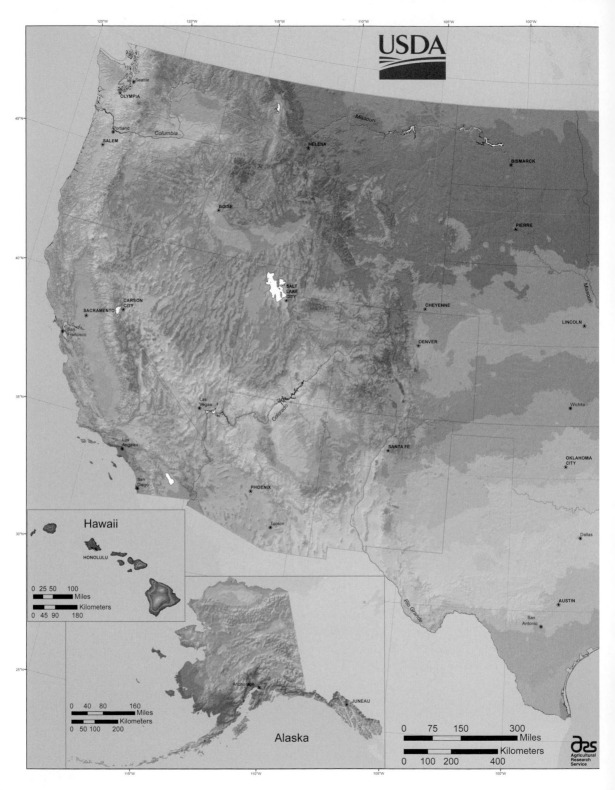

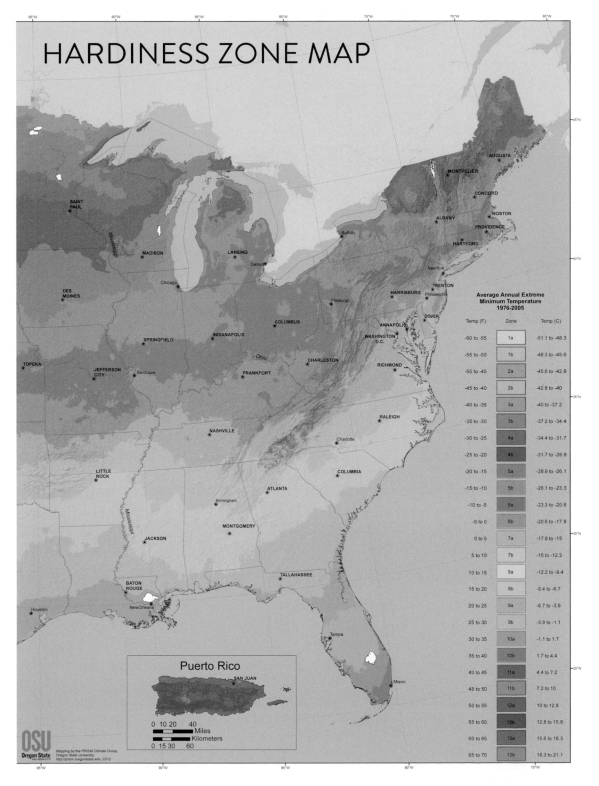

HARDINESS ZONE MAP

Average Annual Extreme Minimum Temperature 1976-2005

Temp (F)	Zone	Temp (C)
-60 to -55	1a	-51.1 to -48.3
-55 to -50	1b	-48.3 to -45.6
-50 to -45	2a	-45.6 to -42.8
-45 to -40	2b	-42.8 to -40
-40 to -35	3a	-40 to -37.2
-35 to -30	3b	-37.2 to -34.4
-30 to -25	4a	-34.4 to -31.7
-25 to -20	4b	-31.7 to -28.9
-20 to -15	5a	-28.9 to -26.1
-15 to -10	5b	-26.1 to -23.3
-10 to -5	6a	-23.3 to -20.6
-5 to 0	6b	-20.6 to -17.8
0 to 5	7a	-17.8 to -15
5 to 10	7b	-15 to -12.2
10 to 15	8a	-12.2 to -9.4
15 to 20	8b	-9.4 to -6.7
20 to 25	9a	-6.7 to -3.9
25 to 30	9b	-3.9 to -1.1
30 to 35	10a	-1.1 to 1.7
35 to 40	10b	1.7 to 4.4
40 to 45	11a	4.4 to 7.2
45 to 50	11b	7.2 to 10
50 to 55	12a	10 to 12.8
55 to 60	12b	12.8 to 15.6
60 to 65	13a	15.6 to 18.3
65 to 70	13b	18.3 to 21.1

Puerto Rico

SAN JUAN

0 10 20   40
Miles
Kilometers
0 15 30   60

OSU
Oregon State
UNIVERSITY

Mapping by the PRISM Climate Group,
Oregon State University,
http://prism.oregonstate.edu, 2012

PHOTOGRAPHY CREDITS

David Austin Roses: 10 (left), 33, 57, 69, 73, 81, 90, 211

Cathy Wilkinson Barash: ii–iii, 183, 227, 236

Helen Battersby: 74, 77, 133 (center), 160

Pam Beck: 60, 98

Trudy Broussard: 65

Marguerite Brown: 66

Sue Brown: 89

Janet Davis: 49, 135, 179, 192, 203

Lynn Hunt: 37, 41, 45, 46, 63, 70, 97, 102, 196, 254

Tom Mayhew: 105

M. J. McCabe: 17

Dawn Miller (© courtesy of Weeks Roses): iv–v, 10 (center), 18, 55, 85, 109, 110, 116

Nancy J. Ondra: vi–1, 3, 4, 5, 7, 8 (bottom), 9, 10 (right), 13, 22, 35, 82, 94, 106, 120, 121, 122, 124, 125, 126, 127, 128, 129, 130, 131, 132 (all), 133 (left and right), 136, 139, 140, 143, 144, 147, 148, 151, 152, 155, 156, 159, 167, 168, 171, 175, 176, 180, 184, 187, 188, 191, 195, 199, 200, 204, 207, 208, 212, 215, 216, 219, 220, 223, 224, 228, 231, 232, 239, 240

Carol Sandt: 8 (top), 42, 58, 113

Shutterstock: 101, 163, 164, 235

Mark Turner: 21, 86

Doreen Wynja: i, 11 (left and right), 14, 25, 26, 30, 38, 50, 53, 78, 93, 114, 172, 244

Doreen Wynja for Monrovia: 11 (center), 29

COVER:

Background photo © Depositphotos.com

Photos on left, from top to bottom: © Nancy J. Ondra, © Nancy J. Ondra, © Doreen Wynja, © Nancy J. Ondra

INDEX